Folk Architecture in Little Dixie

D1233456

Folk Architecture in Little Dixie

A REGIONAL CULTURE IN MISSOURI

Howard Wight Marshall

University of Missouri Press
Columbia & London, 1981

Copyright © 1981 by The Curators of the University of Missouri
Library of Congress Catalog Card Number 80–26064
Printed and bound in the United States of America
University of Missouri Press, Columbia, Missouri 65211

Library of Congress Cataloging in Publication Data

Marshall, Howard Wight
    Folk Architecture in Little Dixie:
    A Regional Culture in Missouri

    Bibliography: p. 128
    1. Vernacular architecture—Missouri
—Little Dixie. I. Title.
NA730.M82L55   728′.67′09778   80–26064
ISBN 0–8262–0329–9

Frontispiece photograph of Locust Grove Farm,
Randolph County, ca. 1950, Marshall family album.

Contents

For Linda
For the Bradley, Marshall, Wight, and Jennings families
And for the people of Missouri

Preface

This study is about material culture and settlement history in a very interesting place and time. Its focus is on the people and the understated voice of their architecture of tradition. Its viewpoint borrows from the fields of geography, archaeology, and history, as well as from my own profession, folklife studies. Like Charles van Ravenswaay's exploration of Germanic material culture in Missouri, this is a book about how folk artifacts help define and illustrate settlement history and cultural regions.

For the theories underlying this book, I have drawn on the work of many different thinkers who have influenced me—a motley crew of folklorists, archaeologists, geographers, anthropologists, and architectural historians. Henry Glassie has been the most sustaining source of usable ideas. His published thought has played a major role in setting field studies of regional material culture in their proper position as a major subfield of folklife and anthropology. Glassie's *Folk Housing in Middle Virginia* provides all architecture specialists with fresh strategies for understanding the ways folk builders create historic buildings. I have noted his formulations, based on structuralism and linguistics, of *competence* ("the ability to compose") and its resulting *performance* ("the product that can be observed by the scholar"), though my stress is more upon the performance of the Little Dixie farmers and carpenters—their architectural achievement in the newly forged cultural landscape of the nineteenth-century Midwest.[1]

This study is in essence exploratory. It does not attempt to completely describe the whole of Little Dixie culture or architecture. It is, rather, a long essay of several parts which will, I hope, by introducing the region and the architecture for the first time in book form, serve as a stimulation and basis for further and more extensive fieldwork and discussion. Much of this study is historical in mood, and the artifacts are clearly "historic buildings." The cutoff date for the buildings documented is 1930, since after this time an assortment of factors began to change the way most people thought a new house should look.

Little Dixie is a cultural region in Missouri composed of eight counties and a vague periphery settled in the early nineteenth century by emigrants from a few southern states, mostly of British stock. Patterns in traditional building, discovered directly by field documentation, furnish an index to regional personality and can help us understand the transplantation of old ideas to new environments. The southern character of Little Dixie is visible in many ways—in the dominance of the Democratic party; in aspects of the social order, world view, and folk culture—and is visible most clearly in the old "southern" countryside of farms and farm buildings. In the architectural evidence behind my definition of the extent of Little Dixie, there are frequencies of certain building "types" (and "styles") and a preference for certain modes of log construction. These patterns of building mirror the region's identification as an island of upland southern folk culture in the lower Midwest with ties of history and mood to Virginia, the Carolinas, and Bluegrass Kentucky that are enormously important to many of the settlers' descendants today.

Studies of folk architecture in the South and East by many researchers—notably by geographer Fred Kniffen and folklorist Henry Glassie—show the usefulness of architectural patterns in the study of a people's history. For Missouri, van Ravenswaay's powerful work gives us information about the German settlers and their material culture along an important stretch of the Missouri River that coincidentally matches Little Dixie's southern perimeter, and my study complements van Ravenswaay's treatise, though it differs in scope and method. The Little Dixie study makes broad use of oral testimony gained in interviews, has a special design and goal underlying the field research at its core, and uses architecture alone as the vehicle of analysis and discussion of cultural meanings and regional personality.

Artifacts often reveal deep meanings about cultural process and the retention of old ways of thought. For the world of buildings, there is perpetual confusion over what "folk architecture" is, and I will explain my theory in a following chapter. Even for folklorists there is conflict over the terms, but most of us in America prefer *folk architecture* as the term of scholarly discourse. The alternate term *vernacular architecture* has broader compass than *folk*, and my Little Dixie research is distinctly with folk buildings as the basis for determining the cultural mix of an area. Furthermore, this study was restricted almost completely to buildings in the rural landscape. Little Dixie is, first of all, a farmer's region. And, importantly, the countryside represents the starting point for folk architectural documentation, just as the countryside was where the settlers settled. The towns came later. Students of folk culture are certainly interested in *both* urban and rural life. But, as with the first folk architectural studies in Britain, the rural cradle of this agricultural region is the logical focus.[2]

   Folk culture is tenacious, and in Little Dixie the southern architectural forms held sway despite German immigration and settlement by
northerners and easterners following the Civil War. The later settlers
were in certain ways easily assimilated into the established order (in certain ways they were not, as in religion and food customs), and the early
types of architecture brought from Virginia and Kentucky and North
Carolina continued to be favored by farmers and builders. Folk architecture does not necessarily "recapitulate demographic research,"[3] but in
Little Dixie the facts of initial settlement and the architecture closely
coincide. The existence of Missouri's Little Dixie is now well known and
has been recognized in popular and academic fashion.[4] Richard Dorson
knew of Little Dixie in 1959 and knew that there was some sort of "sub-
cultural entity or enclave" here that might be an authentic folk region.[5]
Among the few scholarly writings dealing directly with Little Dixie are
those by geographer Robert M. Crisler, whose dissertation years ago
was based on the region and who searched out printed references and
sampled opinions of politicians, newspaper editors, and businessmen.[6] A
volume of fine rustic verse by Albert Trombley, *Little Dixie*, represents
the area in popular literature, and references to Little Dixie occasionally
appear in local media and news stories. Though they do not speak of
"Little Dixie" by name, Henry Belden's classic compilation of Missouri
folksongs many years ago includes material from these counties, Robert
Ramsay's book includes dialect materials, and R. P. Christeson recently
edited a good volume of traditional fiddle music, some of which is Little
Dixie material.[7]

   If it can be shown that Little Dixie dwellings and agricultural buildings reveal southern character, and that these artifacts are an ingredient
in the people's polished image of their area, such firsthand information
will extend our knowledge of informal history and architecture and will
help complete the record of the sources and development of modern
America.

   This book shows a selection of the buildings that I believe to be
representative of the overall architectural configuration of Little Dixie.
My strategy was to record a hundred or so folk buildings across the
counties that I theorized were Little Dixie and to find out how the
people felt about the structures and about the identity of their self-
named region. I then used this ethnographic information in rendering
my particular definition of Little Dixie and in suggesting its meaning in
cultural history. Among the questions that taunted and excited me were:
What motivates a farmer's choice of structural design? When the barn or
house has been built, how does it infuse a family's life with special mean-

ings? Further, how do constellations of traditional buildings infuse the landscape with special meanings—and vice versa? What is important are the emerging *patterns*, and particular groups of patterns form cultural-geographic regions. Little Dixie is very much an *insider's* region, and my work proved fascinating in the testing of hard objective evidence against the people's subjective use of place and their feelings of "region."

Little Dixie exists, of course, and by presenting its architecture in this book I hope to bring these structures to the attention of those who have usually shunned the supposedly ordinary shelters of supposedly ordinary people. Architectural historians often ignore folk buildings unless they have some association with significant historical events, places, or leaders. And when folk buildings are studied, they are too often described as simple, "naive," or "primitive" dwellings cobbled together by some imaginary oafish but fiesty pioneers.

There is an exciting new interest in what has usually been thought of as humdrum, even boring, architecture and cultural expression in the rural Missouri countryside. A good federal effort to record folk buildings in a section of the Clarence Cannon Reservoir flood area in Monroe County was undertaken by the Historic American Buildings Survey (HABS) in the summer of 1978. The "Perry, Missouri Survey" recording team was directed by John Poppeliers and Ken Anderson of HABS in cooperation with the St. Louis District of the Army Corps of Engineers, which is required by federal legislation to pay a small amount (1 percent) of its total project budget for "mitigation" studies in project "impact areas." The work produced would have been radical a few years ago, for the team of field-workers found and studied a good sample of the total corpus of folk buildings and not just the grand Georgian and Victorian mansions we have been led to elevate to highest "significance." Karen Platz Hunt of Bethel has recorded many structures over recent years that will be destroyed by the reservoir, which will not only take the prime Salt River bottomland out of production, but will also obliterate whole towns like Victor and Stoutsville and literally hundreds of important historic buildings throughout the vicinity of the corps project. It is important that outfits like HABS and the Historic American Engineering Record (HAER) are turning their attention toward everyday artifacts that represent the great majority of historic material culture in the United States.[8] It is a kind of salvage research, but it is critical work indeed since it is one kind of preservation: preservation through documentation of these "cultural resources."

The seeds for this seemingly new attention to folk architecture were sown by many hands. Carl Ortwin Sauer's breakthrough historical geography of the Ozarks in 1920 includes information on architecture; the great early collectors of "folklore" in Missouri noted material culture;[9] van Ravenswaay was seriously studying the German communities forty years ago; and there are references to and illustrations of folk buildings scattered throughout dozens of local histories, newspaper stories, student research papers and theses, private photograph collections, state archives, and family histories. Much of this new awareness of the real depth and importance of ordinary rural buildings came with the establishment of the Missouri State Park Board's statewide survey of sites of historical, archaeological, and architectural importance. The Columbia office began noticing folk buildings along with grand academic courthouses in the late 1960s and started speaking of folk architecture as significant to the cultural history and development of the community and region and as worth listing on the National Register of Historic Places. We have finally come to the point where the once-austere HABS regards "significance" in terms of the people in the community as well as in terms of formal, elitist written history. Today at the University of Missouri a new batch of students is embracing the revisionist editorials of folklorists, architectural historians, and preservationists who have found a talented audience of field-workers to take the challenge of recording the unrecorded.

As in Britain,[10] depopulation of the rural areas and towns is a chief cause of the loss of old buildings in the area of Little Dixie, and here the clip at which nineteenth-century houses vanish—through natural reclamation or to man's machines—is as frightening as in the old country where few ancient buildings remain. A change in a house's function, from dwelling place for people to storage for a soybean crop or corn harvest, staves off for a while the inevitable end. But quite simply it is we who choose, very logically, to move up to modernity by constructing a red brick ranch-style house in front of or on the spot where the old, old house once stood. That sort of attempt to change with the fashions of the times is nothing new; what we may herald today as a noble historic house is often the second or third one built on a single farm, and we know nothing of its precursors. Big farms and agribusiness keep engulfing small, marginally profitable farms, too, and this means deep social change for the farmer and his family, who may move into Columbia or Kansas City or St. Louis, live in a tract house, and find new employment. The forces of agribusiness are influential, and it is clear that the old-time family farm we know and hold dear from *Saturday Evening Post* covers is falling victim to the industrial and economic circumstances of the modern age. The progressive spirit and technical savvy of agricultural scientists, manufacturers, government agencies, and the great American tinkerers build on the old ways of life and work, and it is unfortunate that certain of the old ways die. Even unintentionally, current modes of efficient technology make it simpler and eventually cheaper to replace a rackety log corncrib with a galvanized metal bin. And Little Dixie farmers today have little need for the huge transverse-crib barns of the nineteenth century, since the techniques of hay harvest and storage render most of them obsolete. Many old barns and haylofts built for loose hay are now used to store baled hay, but the sheer weight and pressure of modern hay bales cause old timbers to sag and walls to tremble. Further, we tend to replace an old thing rather than bother about its repair or restoration. There seems to be, as W. G. Hoskins says, an insatiable "modern lust for destruction" that in the course of urbanizing the countryside blasts away memory and protective planning.

For the moment, saying this much will do: we must save the spirit of the land and the people, for the future and for ourselves. Our challenge is, as Henry Glassie has often asserted, to "rescue from anonymity" the people and their cultural landscapes in order to achieve a more authentic American history. It is my hope that this book will help do that by presenting actual field documentation of the genius of rural Missouri architecture.

I have not attempted to write a meticulously technical treatise on the construction of buildings. Many of us who study old houses do so in order to learn more about the people who build and use them, and about the processes as well as the end products of tradition. Still, I will be glad if Charles W. Marshall and Walter W. Boswell—one a good carpenter by experience and the other a good carpenter by profession— think that the explanations are suitable. I began learning about architecture the way every child born on a farm does—by meeting the playful then frightening vastness of a big hayloft at sundown, by feeling the dimensions of a muddy hog pen in order to know how much distance I needed to race away from nervous sows with pigs, by learning that the front parlor was a special place for "company" and for listening to my grandmother's piano behind my grandfather's violin on Sunday afternoons after church. If I am a student of rural architecture, I should tell you that I am a biased one. This is the Little Dixie of my youth, and it has been my family's home since the 1830s. Three of my great-great-grandfathers were farming in Randolph County before 1840 and came from the classic source areas: a Marshall from the Virginia Piedmont, a Bradley from the North Carolina Piedmont, and a Wight from the Kentucky Bluegrass.

Why is Little Dixie different? Where is Little Dixie? Can it be drawn out cooly on the grids of a map or does it live only in the selective, passionate recollections of the old farmer and county oracle? Does it exist only for local politicians stumping for the "Democrat ticket?" Does the existence of Little Dixie Eggs, Little Dixie Ham, a Little Dixie State Lake, a Little Dixie CB Radio Club, a Little Dixie square-dance group (The Little Dixie Squares), a Little Dixie Regional Library System, and other public manifestations and iconic uses of the term prove Little Dixie? Those things refer us to a living, vital place that grew from within, not one invented by historians, civic clubs, or journalists.

Acknowledgments

It is impossible to list everyone who helped me in this work, but some ought to be named. As an undergraduate at the University of Missouri, where I returned after three years in the Marine Corps, I was inspired by Osmund Overby, Tom Cooke, and James Holleran, who saw some potential in my early field trips and encouraged me to pursue folk cultural studies. A part-time job with the State Historical Survey and Planning Office in Columbia gave me more field experience and the chance to wedge folk architecture into the state's historic preservation plans. More recently, Overby has been interested in this study and agreed to read it. At Indiana University and since those graduate-school days, my mentor and friend Henry Glassie has been consistently helpful, and I learned much from Dick Dorson, Warren Roberts, Edson Richmond, and Linda Dégh. John Vlach, Tom Adler, Betsy Adler, Bill Lightfoot, Archie Green, and Bill Moore helped with their criticisms. Glassie introduced me to Fred Kniffen in Virginia in 1974, and that conversation and the correspondence that followed helped convince me that the work could be useful. The various writings of Kniffen and Glassie were the chief influence on me during the undergraduate days of sorting out material folk culture and my commitment to folklore as a profession. Ronald W. Brunskill, Carl Condit, Peter Goss, David Stanley, and Dell Upton were helpful in developing my own propositions of what folk architecture is and means. My students at George Washington University asked tough questions that led to some fine tuning. Conversations with James Deetz, Osmund Overby, and Alan Gailey were helpful as the book was moving toward its last version. For my colleagues and students, and finally for Glassie, here are some "small things remembered"—the old buildings that gave and now give meaning to everyday life in Little Dixie.

Of the people across the region who welcomed my abrupt and quizzical tramps through their parlors and yards, I want to list these: Miss Eula Baker, Mrs. Robert W. Leavene, and Walter W. Boswell, Moberly; Earl Westfall, Higbee; Mr. and Mrs. Guy Patton and Mrs. Lue Lozier, Milton; Louis J. Weinhaus, Mt. Airy; Mrs. Jim Klink, Huntsville; Mr. and Mrs. Bill Creson, Yates; Clifton Kivett, Boonesboro; Miss Myrtle VanCourt and Mr. and Mrs. Harold B. Schofield, Hallsville; Mrs. Ben Morris, Centralia; William Orien Wade, Woodlandville; Christy Burks, Rocheport; Fred Hoevelman, Hartsburg; Jake Griffin, Ashland; Mrs. Endemien Pearsall, Stoutsville; Sam Smith, Perry; Carl T. Bounds, Paris; Ralph Gregory, Florida; Kerry Tate, Portland; and Andy Cave, Dixie. Many family members were helpful, including my father, Charles Wiley Marshall of Vancouver, Washington; Mr. and Mrs. James Augustine Wight, Mr. and Mrs. Thomas Jennings Marshall, and my mother, Frances Jennings Marshall, Moberly. In the final job of putting the manuscript in order in 1979, my brother Tom set me up in the Victorian library of his brick central-hall I house in Moberly. My incomparable wife, Linda, aided me in countless ways, and the boys, Sandy and John D., interrupted my writing fits only when they found it necessary for the family's sanity. Linda's parents, Dr. and Mrs. Thomas G. Duckett, were encouraging and helpful in important ways, and some of the writing was done in the quiet basement library of their Georgian house in Hiawatha, Kansas.

H. W. M.
Alexandria, Virginia
September 1980

1
Little Dixie Emerges:
Democrats and Old Slave Days

It's the heart of Missouri, blooded of three,
Virginia, Kentucky, and Tennessee.
It's a tall spare man on a blue-grass hoss.
It's a sugar-cured ham without raisin sauce.
It's coon dog, coon, persimmon tree.
It's son or brother named Robert E. Lee.
It's tiger stalking a jay-hawk bird.
It's the best hog-calling that you ever heard.
It's fiddler fiddlin' you out of your seat,
Fiddler fiddlin' you off your feet.
It's a bluebird singing in a hawthorn thicket.
It's vote to a man the Democratic ticket.
It's crisp brown cracklins' and hot corn-pone.
It's catfish fried clean off the bone.
It's hominy grits and none of your scrapple.
It's mellow pawpaws and the Jonathan Apple.
It's sorghum sweetenin' and belly-warming corn.
It's old Jeff Davis a-blowin' on his horn.
Unreconstructed it rares and bites
At touch of a rein that would curb its rights.
It's come in stranger, draw up a chair;
There ain't no hurry and we'll all get there.[1]

History and the Land

Little Dixie is the world with your county in the middle. Less passionately, Little Dixie is a folk region in north-central Missouri made up of Boone, Howard, Randolph, Audrain, Monroe, Callaway, Pike, and Ralls counties and a transition zone that takes in parts of neighboring counties (Figure 1–1). The area comprises forest and rich farmland and is bounded by major rivers—the Missouri on the south and the Mississippi on the east. The western border of Little Dixie is hazy, and some people there believe the region extends to the Kansas City area. Furthermore, there may be an identifiable Little Dixie in the Joplin area (on

Missouri's far southwest border with Kansas), and other "little Dixies" are known in the far western United States.

The state of Missouri is usually divided into four physiographic regions—the Ozark Highlands, the Southeast Lowlands, the Western Plains, and the Northern Plains.[2] Little Dixie lies in the rolling land of the Northern Plains, geographically and culturally between the Ozarks and the corn belt. Archaeologists who study early native American occupancy in this section of the state call it the Northeast Prairie region and have determined that there were Early Man habitations here at least ten thousand years ago. In historic times, following the first French encounters with the Indians in the eighteenth century, the dominant tribes were the Osage and the Missouri, settled groups with basic hunting and gathering traditions who, with peripheral tribes like the Shawnee, Dela-

Figure 1–1A. The eight counties that compose Missouri's Little Dixie are (1) Boone, (2) Howard, (3) Randolph, (4) Monroe, (5) Audrain, (6) Callaway, (7) Pike, and (8) Ralls. Originally, I used a "test" Little Dixie that included only the first six counties based on Robert Crisler's "An Experiment in Regional Delimitation," an excellent study club paper by Eula Baker (who was a good local historian and lifelong resident), and my 1971 field survey. As I conducted my fieldwork, that test region gave way to an expanded and qualified one and grew to include Pike and Ralls counties and a peripheral zone of transition around the main eight counties.

ware, Kickapoo, and Sac and Fox, were gradually displaced westward throughout the eighteenth and first half of the nineteenth century.[3] Northeast Missouri, part of which is Little Dixie domain today, was the hunting territory of the Sac and Fox Indians, and there was a good deal of interchange, both good and bad, between the Indians and the incoming American settlers.

The region was settled initially and effectively by hunters and then farmers from certain lowland areas of upland southern states—Kentucky, Virginia, Tennessee, and the Carolinas. The southerners were well suited to the new environment, which was much like Bluegrass Kentucky and Virginia's Piedmont from the Blue Ridge Mountains down into the Tidewater. Their architecture was generally accepted and added to by the Germans (who built "English" house *types* but kept their own massive barn types as the centerpieces of farmsteads), northerners, and easterners. The people's own vision of Little Dixie is based on two main things: first, on a "southern" past (which some call "the old slave days") of to-

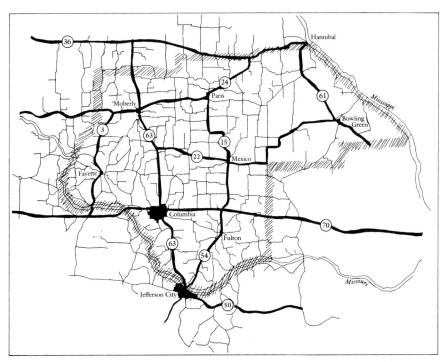

Figure 1–1B. An intricate system of planned traverses by automobile was employed in order to obtain an intensive coverage of Little Dixie and the peripheral counties. On the map, the main highways (mostly U.S. highways connecting main towns) are darkened; the lighter lines indicate state and county roads covered in the field research. The diagonal hatching shows the edges of the Little Dixie region's chief area.

Figure 1–2. Mrs. Anna Bernice Vernon of Sturgeon, Boone County, paints scenes from her family's history such as this one, titled *Migrating to Missouri* (April 1974).

bacco farms, log houses, country ham, fox hunts, rail fences, "old southern mansions" (only remotely like the famous manor houses on big Deep South plantations), and what they imagine to have been a more genteel life-style, and second, on the overwhelming dominance of the Democratic party in local politics.

The southerners came into central Missouri on foot, on horseback, and by mover wagon (Figure 1–2). The migrants came in two main stages: first, the adventurous frontiersmen-hunters-trappers, who practiced minimal subsistence farming, and second, the permanent yeomen farmers. This land beyond the Mississippi had a strong attraction. The soils and climate were familiar to the immigrants, and slaves could be used for labor on the farms. Missouri's chief source of population was those upper south states, and most settlers were actually from lowland sections—the Bluegrass, the Tidewater-Piedmont, and the Nashville basin.[4] Many farmers brought their slaves, tobacco, horses, and hemp plants and settled in the region north of the Missouri, while the so-called mountaineers from highland parts of the same southern states tended to settle south of the river in the hill country of the Ozarks. The newcomers who laid out the farms and towns of Little Dixie were almost entirely of British background, both Anglo-Americans from the southern states and more recent British immigrants who had passed through these same areas on their way to Missouri.

In religious practice, these settlers represented the dominant Protestant denominations: they were primarily Methodists, Baptists, Disciples of Christ, Presbyterians, and Episcopalians.[5] Though Missouri was largely Roman Catholic during French occupancy and rule before 1804, and though many Germans (both Lutherans and Catholics) settled later in Little Dixie, the French had left few traces on the virgin territory, and the Germans, coming after the Anglo-Americans, had tended to settle on the margins and in pockets in the early days of permanent settlement before the Civil War. Rural Little Dixie remains a Protestant stronghold today, just as it remains a stronghold for conservative political values and traditions of self-reliance and deep family ties. The influence of the rural Protestant churches peaked in the 1890s, at the same time that other aspects of rural life reached their zenith, such as success for small family farms and the flourishing of impressive Victorian-styled folk farmhouses.

It is remembered by Little Dixie Missourians today that their ancestors stopped and stayed not only because of the availability of new farmland, but also, as Jim Wight of Randolph County and many other people say, because "it looked just like Kentucky." The settlers were culturally preadapted to the new lands and selected ground that was indeed familiar to what they had known. The familiar-looking earth was often not the most productive land, but it was the best land of the desired type available. It was later discovered that this good-looking gray dirt in the area's floodplains and grasslands was tough "prairie topsoil" and difficult to plow and cultivate. The development of the self-polishing steel plows that could move through the sticky, heavy soils in the 1830s and 1840s made ground breaking easier. Little Dixie even had "bluegrass." Howard County looked so much like home that it was called "little Virginia," though oddly there is no "little Kentucky" here. A glance at place names shows the southern imprint. The notion of Kentucky as the "mother of Missouri" lingers on and is kept current by Kentucky names on the landscape.[6]

It took several years after Boone's travels for the Missouri Territory to gain much population, but steady streams of settlers began moving to the area after the War of 1812. Kentucky, Virginia, Tennessee, and the Carolinas "drained many of their new communities" into Missouri and, by 1850, Kentucky had sent nearly seventy thousand immigrants.[7] Before 1803, when it was purchased by Thomas Jefferson as part of the

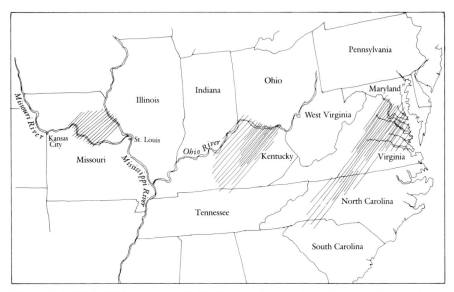

Figure 1–3. Little Dixie was settled chiefly by emigrants from Virginia, the Carolinas, and Kentucky.

Louisiana Territory, Missouri had been Spanish and then French territory, but in forty years of rule the Spanish left little trace, while the Missouri region was really French only along the rivers. French farmers had black slaves as early as 1720 in Missouri, and both they and the Spanish kept Indian slaves. The Spanish built no towns and no roads in the Little Dixie region, and their impact was felt only slightly along the river trade routes. French influence along the Mississippi is well documented; their fine houses built of vertical logs in the *poteaux en terre* and *poteaux sur sole* methods with catted chimneys and gallery porches and their well-organized towns using the European open-field system are well known. But out away from St. Louis they left little impression, and by 1810 the French colors were fading. The War of 1812 resulted in the demise of the fur trade, and at war's end in 1815, new settlement from the South—Anglo-America—"became a tidal wave."[8]

Like the rest of the territory, the central and east-central parts experienced a huge surge in settlement in the post–War of 1812 era. There were two main routes to the region from Kentucky and Virginia. The first was a land route across southern Indiana and Illinois that entered Missouri by crossing the Mississippi River north of St. Louis. The second was a land-and-water route that either entered Missouri at St. Louis or crossed the Mississippi below its junction with the Missouri. Those who followed the latter route also had to cross the Missouri at some point west, such as Franklin, Boonville, or Glasgow. In one case, the Creson family came to Howard County in the fall of the year by the southerly route and had to wait until the winter weather froze the turbulent Missouri before they could cross on the ice near Boonville.

> *Marshall:* Did you tell me one time that your grandfather came from North Carolina?
> *Bill Creson:* Yup, North Carolina. In a covered wagon. And they waited till the river froze over and crossed it on the ice. Wasn't no other crossing. Crossed it on the ice.

Mrs. Marshall's narrative describes the land route used by her great-grandfather, Capt. James F. R. Wight, and something of the early settlement phase:

> Well, they must have come as part of the western movement—just a desire to go west on their own. . . . They came from Shelby County, Kentucky, as Methodists, and continued their religion here. The desire to move west. They came as far as Randolph County. They loved the country here, because it looked much like Kentucky to them. And if you look at the names in this area, in the county, so many of the names are directly copied from the state they came from. They came in 1836. The thing I remember best from family traditions is the fact that when they arrived here they had rescued thirteen babies and young children that had been abandoned from Indian raids—and old Captain Wight reared all these thirteen children as his own. . . . The first winter here was particularly hard—very difficult,

Figure 1–4. Mules. Randolph County, Missouri, ca. 1920. Private collection.

because they were not prepared for it. The cabins were very rude, with only a parchment paper over the windows for glass, and skins up over the doors. . . . The land had to be cleared, and I suppose it was a terrible job to get set up and take care of a family. . . . They came over from Kentucky in mover wagons, driven by oxen.[9]

Such accounts of local history are abundant and important to old-timers in Little Dixie. In the logic and the world view of many of the settlers, history is simple: first there was old Boone and his boys Nathan and Daniel Morgan, and the Indians; then there was grandfather laying out the farm; then there was the Civil War and the "thievin' Yankees"; and now, there's us.

The county histories and travelers' accounts of Missouri do not mention the term *Little Dixie*, and only one of the modern histories of Missouri mentions Little Dixie by name.[10] County histories and travel literature offer eloquent but often romantic impressions of olden times, painted in loving or malicious strokes.[11] For the cultural historian these fascinating yet incomplete histories provide much food for thought, and for the folk-culture researcher they often provide accurate appraisals of early life and work as well as commentaries on the building of log houses or on the reasons for settling at the edges of deep forests rather than in the natural open spaces. Some of the old county histories are helpful in demonstrating Little Dixie's source areas. For example, Alexander Waller's good 1920 book on Randolph County lists the places of origin of old settlers: 153 from Kentucky, 24 from Virginia, 28 from Tennessee, 19 from North Carolina, and 1 from Maine.[12] In addition, the county histories often describe architecture, house types, and methods of construction.[13]

A people's cultural background influences its emigration plans. Grandfather came from Scotland to Virginia; father pushed on to Kentucky; son pushed on to Missouri, after which the westward push ended for most people. Of course, other factors affected migrational tendencies, such as the political climate of the moment, the current state of the economy, the environment, and individual life-styles. In settlement, the effectiveness of that first moment of arrival depends on the ability of the agricultural technology and the economic organization to meet the challenge of the land. And in the case of Little Dixie, conveniently enough, much of the landscape and climate matched that of the southern areas from which the immigrants came. The agricultural tools and techniques, the supportive craft traditions, and the forms of farm and town planning all traveled well. The period of first effective settlement—from about 1815 to the 1850s—supplied the imprint that later gave meaning to the people's notion that they lived in a place called Little Dixie. The conditions of the new habitat encouraged the keeping of established traditions. The presence of the southern mood is important in the regionalizing process, and a mixing of populations did not really begin until German immigration in the 1840s, and then the impact was mainly along the Missouri River perimeter of the southerners' domain.[14] Dissolution of the original population makeup occurred after the southerners' troubles following the Civil War, with the influx of Yankee settlers empowered by the Reconstruction government and with the increase in the number of skilled German yeomen farmers.

Driving Little Dixie Down

The strong Jacksonian sense of nationhood that bloomed after the War of 1812 ended with the Civil War. In the time when the lower Midwest was taking shape, this turn toward regional feeling in Missouri was sharpened by the ravages inflicted by Northern armies on a border state mostly sympathetic to the losing Confederate cause. Particularly troublesome were those state militiamen who took advantage of their powers to pillage the farms of people who were known or suspected to be "secessionists" or Confederate sympathizers. There are many accounts of the havoc caused by the Missouri federal militia, many of whom were Little Dixie residents. In the oral tradition about the bad times during and after the war, the local militia was more feared than the Union army itself.

> *Mary Creson:* Well, you was talking about the Civil War. Well, my grandfather lived in the house that joins on the east. And so when they come, . . . they just placed their guns around the butt of the tree, and went into the house and made them prepare food. And they took the hams, and some instances they took quilts. . . . 'Course it was fall, and cold weather coming on. But they just taken *everything* they wanted.

> *Bill Creson:* Well, when they'd come to yer place, they'd take everything off the table you had t'eat. Didn't leave nothing. Pretty hard times.

> *Mary Creson:* Well—people were glad to divide, but it looked awful hard that they took *all* that they had. 'Cause when they had t'work and raise, and do without to accomplish something for themselves.

There is something in the plundering of neighbors that is not forgotten.

> *John Wells:* The Yankee militia—just a bunch of durn *thieves* is what they were. Stole everything. They'd go to the meat house and just clean it out. Ole Jeff Jones got up some kind of treaty with 'em to stay outa Callaway County, and that's where they got the name Little Dixie. . . . Militia weren't regular Union soldiers, they was just a bunch o' thieves down from

Wellsville. Why they wouldn't even wait till night—they'd go out and get that stuff in broad daylight.

And many remained bitter about the treatment their families had received:

> *Clarence Klink:* Bushwhackers? They was the *scums of the Union army.* They come to the house one night and held a shovel of hot coals over dad's head trying to make grandpaw tell 'em where their money was hid. They didn't tell, so the bushwhackers spread the hot coals around the cabin floor. Paw got the fire put out after they left.[15]

Some Little Dixie families had secret storage chambers built into their houses for keeping valuable documents, possessions, and cash money; called "hidey-holes," these places were the responsibility of the woman of the house, who alone knew their location. In moments of crisis (during an unexpected raid by marauders or militia), she often passed the hidey-hole's location on to her eldest daughter or, if need be, the eldest son.

Figure 1–5. Confederate Guerrilla. Marshall family album.

The sad memories that remain about the militia result from the occasional brutality of these forces, sometimes called "the pawpaw militia" after that bitter-tasting fruit.[16] The local militia had outfits posted across the state and tried to keep order and assist the regular Union troops with small campaigns. The militia protected supply trains and "constantly set out patrols on 'search and destroy' missions. In many cases the enemy forces were outlaws and desperadoes, rather than units operating under . . . orders; consequently the rules of war were not always observed by either side."[17]

It was not just the Yankee victors who terrified the inhabitants of Little Dixie; southerners there were equally afraid of the renegade Confederate marauders. "Bloody Bill" Anderson was a Huntsville boy, and no one was proud of his terrible raids of slaughter and pillage across Missouri. Anderson and his tough band, though often operating under legitimate orders from the Confederate command, are sometimes remembered as "scalawags" and "yellow-bellied yahoos."[18] Some southerners' family albums contain a soiled tintype of a young "black sheep" with rakish moustache and cradled Colt Navy revolver who rode with Anderson or George Todd or with Capt. William Clarke Quantrill in desperate efforts to help the Confederate armies, and themselves (Figure 1–5).

Much of the hatred leveled at the southerners in Missouri was due to their status as slaveholders, whether particular treatment of black slaves was good or bad, and this became a logic for justifying the actions of the rapacious Reconstruction government. Indians had earlier been impressed as agricultural laborers by the Spanish and then by the French, and many southerners migrated to Missouri because of its official openness to slavery, which became legal under the Missouri Compromise of 1820. Black slaves were used as fieldhands and as "houseworkers," and many were kept peaceable with threats of being "sold down South" where the treatment of slaves was known to be less favorable.[19] As in the South, few farms were large enough to afford the use of many slaves or an overseer, and the 1820 Missouri Constitution provided measures for the slaves' protection. Most farmers kept few slaves, and houseworkers usually had quarters in the farmhouse, most often in a loft over the kitchen at the back of the house, known as the "servant's room." Census reports show that in 1830 there were eleven counties in Missouri with sizable slave populations, and of these, six are in Little Dixie (Boone, Howard, Randolph, Callaway, Pike, and Ralls counties), and two of the other five counties are adjacent to the formal Little Dixie region (Marion and Saline). In Missouri, about an eighth of the white families held slaves, but there were sufficient numbers of slaves that occasional "slave scares" took place in the wake of the intense abolitionist activity in the 1850s on the eve of the war.[20]

Adding to the hostility of the southerners in Missouri after the Civil War were various features of the Reconstruction plans being carried out by President Johnson, which here included the despised "Iron Clad Oath," a loyalty oath that kept former southern sympathizers from holding public office, voting, or teaching school, thus allowing the Radicals to control local affairs. This situation differed from that in both the northern and the southern states during Reconstruction years, because on top of the tottering economy and shaken community structure, in Missouri "Yankee and Rebel had to learn to live together again."[21]

For the old southerner in central Missouri, the jarring combination of post–Civil War events that upset the economy and disfigured the social fabric and the coming of German farmers able to buy the lands of impoverished southerners represented the close of an era that would later be thought of as a "golden age" of prewar Missouri.

There are good accounts of the movement of Germans into central Missouri in the midnineteenth century, and there are numerous descriptions of their frugality and skill in working the land and in building their vast stout barns and farm buildings.[22] Unlike the southerners, the Germans often came because of political disaffection and troubles in their homeland (following the unsuccessful revolutions of 1830 and 1848). Many of the "Forty-Eighters" were unusually well educated and of high social standing, and here as in Pennsylvania they were regarded as "valuable acquisitions" due to their skills and aptitude for the pioneering existence. German farmers were noted for their ability to use every bit of available material and foodstuff, and they often considered their "American" neighbors to be unmotivated (to put it lightly) and wasteful. Germans and Americans were often at odds in central Missouri.

> The wasteful methods of the American pioneer irritated the German farmer. Moreover, he was offended by the temporary nature of the American pioneer farms, for the German looked upon his holding as something permanent. . . . "There is scarcely a farm," wrote a German farmer in Missouri . . . "that is not for sale, for the American farmer has no love for home, such as a German has. I am building a smokehouse, a kitchen, a milk-house over one of the excellent springs near our house, a stable for the horses and one for the cows. My American neighbors say that I am building a town." . . . The American pioneer seemed inexcusably wasteful with all he possessed. . . . The German farmer, on the other hand, seemed to his American neighbors to be inexcusably frugal, materialistic, and penurious.[23]

A humorous passage in a book by James T. Lemon hints that the famous Pennsylvania Germans were not all superfarmers; in 1783 a German farmer there told a traveler that "he would rather live somewhere else, but . . . he had heard that in Kentucky there was no real winter; and where there is no winter, he argued, people must work year in and year out, and that was not his fancy; winter, with a warm stove and sluggish days being indispensable to his happiness." [24] In a more up-to-date appraisal, Charles van Ravenswaay notes that, although "the planter aristocracy remained aloof," the settlers in the new Missouri Rhineland would have had a tough time of it without the general good will of the southerners. [25]

The years before the Civil War and the influx of the German settlers were of course not a true "golden age," but it was a time of promise. The memory of those years evolved into the spirit of Little Dixie. Although no one noticed when or how, the term *Little Dixie* slowly took shape in people's minds as a name for the place in which they lived. The ways in which the now disadvantaged southerners responded to the changed social and economic conditions provided a foundation for later nativistic urges leading to self-awareness and receptivity to the idea of a Little Dixie. Southernness became secondary, but its imprint remained strong in the private cultural systems of food customs, legend cycles, speech patterns, family sagas, and in architecture deriving from old southern traditions embodying principles of Anglo-American building. Internal awareness of the sense of Little Dixie developed first, followed by an external and political awareness. When the vote was restored to southerners in the 1870s, the Democratic party at once took hold both as a logical preference and as an expression of personal feeling. In the regionalizing process by which Little Dixie is best understood as the result and manifestation of old settlement patterns and folk cultural tendencies, the dimension of politics can be added to other factors of regional consciousness.

Little Dixie Democrats

The cultural oppositions resulting from the changes wrought by the Civil War, and especially by Reconstruction, resulted not in a further rending of the social fabric but instead in a mediation of the various political forces. The Democratic party became a gathering point for the southerners in the 1870s and provided the vehicle by which the "old" Missourians regained influence over the state's affairs. The completeness of public dissatisfaction with the Reconstruction government (among southerners and others alike) was powerful. When restoration of voting privileges offered the chance to dislodge carpetbag rule, the people came

Figure 1–6. Farmer, Randolph County, ca. 1860. Marshall family album.

to the support of local leaders, many of whom were southerners, as a means of recapturing self-rule. One such leader in Little Dixie, Capt. James F. R. Wight, was an ex-Kentuckian who had held slaves on his farm near Milton. A "Southern sympathizer," Wight had been congressman from Randolph County in 1854, and he was reelected after the demise of Reconstruction in 1876. Since 1872, residents of the Little Dixie counties have consistently voted for Democratic candidates in both local and national elections.

The best treatment of Little Dixie politics can be found in the work of Robert M. Crisler, which defines the region based on the fascinating political scene. His findings were drawn from the answers given to questions about Little Dixie put to a group of public leaders in the area— businessmen, lawyers, politicians, newspapermen—people considered to have an "objective" and "expert though nonprofessional opinion." Crisler's *Missouri Historical Review* article shows that few people agree on what counties lie within Little Dixie (just as I discovered in my own

Figure 1–7. Missourians. The patriarch from Kentucky, Capt. James Francis Ratcliff Wight (*left rear*) posed at eighty with his successors in October 1899: son James William Wight, fifty-seven, *right rear*; grandson James Winter "Obe" Wight, thirty; and great-grandson James Augustine Wight, four and a half. More than photographic images, such pictures are important artifacts and icons in family history. Marshall family album.

conversations across the area), and that its main regional signal is the Democratic political situation and tradition. Crisler checked election returns and voting habits back to 1872 and found an extremely pronounced "political regionalism" by which the region could be delimited.[26] His political-geographic study twenty-five years ago nicely matches my delimitation of Little Dixie: our eight principal counties coincide, showing the correspondences between the overt political aspects of a region and the less well understood aspects of regional personality like architecture. Politics itself can of course be "regional personality."

"Stump speakings" are a campaign tradition strongly associated with the Democratic party in Missouri, and these events are still a necessary ritual for aspiring politicians, and for old hands as well. Stump speakings are rare elsewhere in the state, and in Little Dixie they carry over from the early days and the heated debates of the 1830s and 1840s between Jacksonian Democrats and Whigs. In these speakings, Democratic candidates ardently remind their listeners that they live in a stronghold of Democracy, and the belief in the effectiveness of the old morality and good will of the party persists so strongly that many voters blithely and confidently continue to vote a straight ticket in the November elections, many unaware that Republicans are even on the slate.[27]

The vision of Little Dixie is kept publicly alive today chiefly by exposure in the media, but such visions operate only with the approval of the local population. If the idea of Little Dixie conjured no warm images in the people, the media and the politicians would seek another, more productive symbol. For now, and very likely for a long time to come, the idea of "Little Dixie" will not only continue to collect Democratic votes come November election time but will also serve as a memory stimulator, a rallying point, and even as a psychic shelter for all sorts of Little Dixie citizens.

2
The Notion of Folk Architecture

In American discourse, *folklife* can be explained as:
> the traditional expressive culture shared within the various groups in the United States: familial, ethnic, occupational, religious, regional. Expressive culture includes a wide range of creative and symbolic forms such as custom, belief, technical skill, language, literature, art, architecture, music, play, dance, drama, ritual, pageantry, and handicraft. Generally, these expressions are learned orally, by imitation, or in performance, and are maintained or perpetuated without formal instruction or institutional direction.[1]

That definition of folklife encompasses more than just a culture's oral literature, which in contemporary scholarship has come to mean oral tradition. Modern folklife researchers try to go beyond past methods of folkloristic inquiry that taught us little about the depth, quality, and context of tradition, to describe and explain (from various theoretical viewpoints) the whole system of mind. *Material culture* is the array of artifacts and cultural landscapes that people create according to traditional, patterned, and often tacit concepts of value and utility that have been developed over time, through use and experimentation. These artifacts and landscapes objectively represent a group's subjective vision of custom and order. Material culture can be viewed even more broadly, and simply, as James Deetz does: it is "that segment of man's physical environment which is purposely shaped by him according to culturally dictated plans."[2] Material culture is the traditional community's world of art and craft. It is the products of tradition.

Folk architecture is a significant component of material culture, and in turn an important component of folklife. Folk architecture includes both the artifacts that shelter people as they go about their daily lives and work and the study of the contexts and processes in which those shelters, the artifacts, are made and used. Folk architecture often depends on locally available materials, and adaptive changes are made when builders build traditional structures in new lands or environments. Writers in different disciplines call the objects and their study by different names. *Folk architecture* and *vernacular architecture* are the two current favorites in the main academic disciplines conducting and publishing research on the subject—folklife (folkloristics), historical archaeology, architectural history, cultural geography, and anthropology. As new work in this growing arena is produced, the results will continually lead us to refine and polish our theories and definitions. Indeed, this is an exciting period in folk architecture research.

Architectural history provides the formal dimensions of date and style that reinforce the academic view of history as composed of gradually successive periods of flourish and innovation. This foreground of academic or elite history often conceals the day-to-day scenes in architecture, which are dotted with buildings the standard books leave out. The formal, exclusive architectural record lists achievements and adventures in creativity. Behind this lie all the rest—the ordinary houses and their builders and users, whose intentions have long suggested the retention of accepted, normative models and the replication of traditional plans and concepts. We are interested in architecture, but particularly in the sorts of buildings planted on the land by average people for their functional requirements, which show little of the schooled architect's influence. But for the folk architecture of Little Dixie, there is not enough formal historical evidence to say much about the region's real architectural personality. Early travelers wrote about the dominance of log cabins and "double houses," but for information today on rural architectural traditions, fieldwork—observation, documentation, explanation—is the key to understanding.

The questions of the folklorist and the questions of the architectural historian are complementary. While formal history presents an impressive chronology of period and innovation, folklife studies veer toward learning about the cultural landscape that harbors mundane buildings and craftsmen working largely within custom, continuity, and regional patterns rather than exploring the horizons of creativity and invention. Folklorists, many historical archaeologists, cultural geographers, and others are in business for many reasons, but among the most common is the ambition to fill in some of the gaps in the official record of American civilization and to define the lines of mental process and cultural behavior in traditional society. Folklife, often a regional concern, is the science of man as a cultural being, and especially of that part of human culture governed and informed by familiar patterns of artistic expression.

Traditional builders adapt old ways to new landscapes in the course of settlement, and as each new land is tampered with by carpenters and masons and farmers a sense of place gradually appears. Regions when effectively settled take on the appearance of possession, and they take on a special character that local citizens come to know and identify with home and community. Architectural patterns are a basic factor in the process of regionalization—like ethnicity, like economics, like language—wherein local landscapes are made. The student of folk buildings has fewer ready sources, lacking the kinds of records that allow for orderly histories of academic architecture. The student of folk buildings must ramble off into the countryside and little towns to examine the constellation of artifacts made by unrecorded craftsmen.

There are really two basic sorts of architecture: "folk" and "academic." Different writers use different labels according to the dictates of their own scholarly fields. A standard definition by architectural historian Cary Carson explains "vernacular" architecture as "a term invented by archaeologists to describe buildings that are built according to local custom to meet personal requirements of the individuals for whom they are intended. Its opposite may be called polite architecture and can be taken to include everything from self-conscious buildings designed by architects or copied from pattern books to unassuming farmhouses, which, nevertheless, are laid out or ornamented to conform to the dictates of the imported taste."[3] In the mainstream *Dictionary of Architecture*, Henry H. Saylor says simply that "vernacular" means "indigenous; characteristic of a locality," and the other popular paperback dictionary, *A Dictionary of Building* by John S. Scott, ignores the subject;[4] most architectural historians agree (as I do) that the local and regional character is important and that vernacular buildings are made usually from locally available materials. Architectural historians tend to use the term *vernacular* instead of *folk* and then oppose it to "polite" (Ronald Brunskill), "high-design" (Carl Condit), "high architecture" (Osmund Overby), "cultivated architecture" (John Kouwenhoven), "fine," "high style," or "academic architecture." Geographers, folklorists, and some anthropologists use *folk architecture* as a synonym for *vernacular*, but vernacular is actually a much broader category. Some folklorists, like Henry Glassie, divide culture into three categories—folk, popular, and elite—and it would follow that there can be folk, popular, and elite architecture. Some anthropologists add a fourth group at the bottom below folk—"primitive" architecture.

All this gets confusing. What is important is the work, not the words. The cleavage between folk and academic architecture is only the scholar's device to cut up reality into studiable chunks. Categories are invented for clarification as well as for classification, and they help us to sharpen our perceptions about people's feelings, methods, and contexts for creating objects or ballads or legends. Despite being the scholar's feeble attempt to understand things by putting them in coded jars, the categories are necessary.

Like other artifacts, buildings may also reflect different primary functions. Some houses are aimed at public taste and approval, and their style dominates their outward appearance. Such houses showing the fanciful strokes of current vogue may or may not be handy to live and work in. Beyond serving as shelter, these houses function to induce admiration and respect in the passer-by and satisfy the ambitions of the owners. Most houses like this (rambling Gothic masterpieces or a startling box of glass by Philip Johnson) are intended to tickle, please, and otherwise affect other designers and buyers. That set is called academic architecture. The other set, where practical use and comfort dominate and partake of community expectations and traditions, is called folk architecture.

But like art and music, architecture is actually one long continuum.[5] When we finally get down to cases, we could place every structure in its place along this continuum. A simple corncrib would find a niche at one end clearly marked "folk architecture," the Wainwright Building in St. Louis would wind up at the far end called "academic architecture," and a 1915 frame pattern-book bungalow would find its spot somewhere in the foggy zone between folk and academic.

Academic architecture moves on the surface of international fashion, with new styles glimmering in the light and changing according to the drawings of the latest Latrobe, Downing, van der Rohe, or Pei. This kind of stylistic design, powered by architects and design schools, moves as the surreal cutting edge of fashion, setting trends that are either accepted or rejected at other levels of society and culture. Folk architecture moves at deeper and calmer levels: slowly, confidently, and at a safe distance from the jarring models of futuristic design. Academic architecture leans toward the future. Folk architecture leans toward memory and custom. Traditional building does not fully accept radical changes, but it often accommodates change by functionally recombining current styles with accepted, traditional forms. There is a continual interchange between these categories of architecture, of course, in both an upward and a downward movement of ideas.

Type versus Style. When the folklorist arranges architectural information, floorplans form the basic element—like the text of a poem—and these measured floorplans can be ordered into a morphology of types based on form. Architectural styles are not the same as architectural types, and some confusion results from the frequent mixing up of the terms or from conscious suppression of the differences between them. Some historians disapprovingly regard folk building typologies as "misleading groupings of buildings that do not belong together in any meaningful way,"[6] while folklorists would think it wrong to classify buildings by details of ornament that do not help us understand the folk cultural

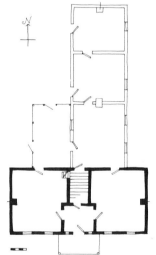

Figure 2–1. The cloak of "style" often overlays folk houses, as in this frame central-hall house in the old town of Stoutsville in Monroe County; outside it looks like a "Gothic cottage" from a builder's guide, but inside the plan is a traditional one.

process or the building's type. Since Campbell's influential house typology that was based on the location of the hearth in the floorplan, scholars have expanded the single feature to include the assemblage of bays, openings, height, and depth. Formal considerations are not only linear (floorplan, location of doors, windows, and chimneys), but they are also vertical and volumetric (height, depth, total space).[7]

Styles in building shift drastically from period to period as a result of both academic innovation and fashion, but the more steady patterns in traditional house and barn design persist over generations. The surface features of a type of house may vary with the application of stylish trim or a decorative gable over the front porch (Figure 2–1), but the house's ideal core—its floorplan—does not change. To the family inside, their house is comfortably traditional in layout and use, while outside the house may have the appearance of the current pattern book. And more than just showing someone's desire to be up-to-date, a house or barn's decorative nuances (more carefully chosen and applied than we suspect) reflect and satisfy a real aesthetic sensibility by which many traditional buildings "transcend the strictly utilitarian."[8] Groups of floorplans constitute a typology that can be studied to evaluate the ethnicity, tradition, and source area of the builders. We then can search through preceding studies to find precedents and early forms from which diffusion or evolution or other forms of influence can be suggested; it is often extremely useful to trace the ways in which old patterns of folk artifacts are transplanted into new regions.[9]

The home is always the center of life and work, and traditional houses display the customs and concepts of their makers at the same time that they shape and take shape from the lives of their inhabitants. These houses can be studied as part of architectural history or as features of the cultural and physical landscape. From local configurations of houses built by different communities at different times, patterns of regional flavor emerge. As with many of the buildings in Little Dixie, researchers often deal with vacant or tumbled-in buildings in order to examine them intensely.

The idea of progress is basic to understanding folk building. Academic architecture is progressive. Folk architecture tends to resist change. Progress to a Little Dixie farmer in the middle of the nineteenth century was putting sash-sawed, lapped horizontal weatherboarding over the walls of his hewn-log house. In addition to the protection offered by the bearing walls and chinking, the weatherboarding represented the farmer's statement toward the fashion for frame construction, however incompletely realized. The siding (often applied at the time of the log house's completion) gave the appearance of a frame building, and the farmer was satisfied. The family kept the interior of the house the way they wanted it, to fit the temper of their private culture, and at the same time their material participation in the public domain was obvious from the road (Figure 2–2). This is progress through accepted channels. It is a process of becoming, not of being current.

The best architecture is that which meets the expectations of the land, as Thoreau said a long time ago, and folk architecture is closely tied to the landscape. Nearly all historic folk buildings are indeed made with the raw materials provided by nature and available close at hand.

Figure 2–2. People in Little Dixie dwell comfortably within tradition and like all of us welcome appropriate or popular innovation *when it jells*. Fancy wood and tin trim were nailed up on the porch of his house to enliven it in the days of Victorian splendor, and years ago Louis J. Wienhaus bought the finest Bacon and Day tenor banjo when the craze hit the Midwest. At the same time that he has modern agricultural equipment today, he still hews out oak logs with a broadax when a mule kicks a chunk out of the old barn's sill and he must replace it. Farm near Mt. Airy, Randolph County.[10]

Of the countless examples, rock bunkhouses in Nevada, adobe houses in New Mexico, Kansas "soddies," and the so-called American log cabin come to mind. Folk culture exists in a direct relationship with the physical environment; it is an ecology of architecture. The cultural landscape itself can be seen as man's most important artifact: the land is molded, shaped, and transformed by us, and the patterns that evolve from working and living on the land express the old closeness of man and nature.[10]

Artifacts are useful to the student of cultural process, for they reveal the maker's intention in his work. Architecture helps us perceive the wavering configuration behind the concrete yet mute artifact.[11] The folk builder or singer or tale teller is an artist, but one who works with different *rules* of art. His perception of value and beauty is different from that of the academic, couched in conservative behavior and expectations. The traditional builder's rules strive for harmony and symmetry rather than inventiveness and fragmentation. Tradition-minded people live within geographic regions and communities that treasure stability, order, replication, balance, and priority and that largely shun jolting novelty.

One of the standard points some commentators make is that folk things are the result of some sort of primitive yet intuitive "unselfconscious" procedure. An example of the sort of condescending, elitist attitude that confuses and mars some popularized presentations of folk architecture is the following by Christopher Williams: "Indigenous architects have found this approach through need. They are not consciously aware of the subtleties of their work; they act naturally and out of simple necessity"; "No written plans are needed, . . . no concern with passing information from one worker to another. . . . Each [product] is fresh and vital, as though it were the only one ever to exist." [12]

Of course there is a good deal of simple construction that seems to have been just thrown up when a farmer struck the right mood, but such considerations are stressed at the cost of looking only at the surface and not at the deeper structure and mental process. People are more "aware" than some of us give them credit for being. In creating or designing folk artifacts, they make calculated decisions based on their knowledge of and opinions about style, type, function, economy, and intention. All forms of art are symbolic representations of philosophy. They are enactments. Whether a philosophy of conservatism and tradition enacted in the little hall-and-parlor house where Sam Clemens was born in Monroe County in 1835 or a philosophy of progress and achievement enacted in W. W. Greenland's towered Victorian mansion in Randolph County, the complex moods of different people are made visible for the world in the houses they choose to erect and dwell in. Folk culture involves a living process of mediation and technical execution as well as the tangible products we see and ponder. If folk builders want "good fit," then conscious, careful decisions are necessary, whether or not they are written down or eloquently explained. Solving the design problem requires fitting form to context (the conditions and possibilities of the local physical and cultural landscape). Christopher Alexander puts it this way, effectively: "every design problem begins with an effort to achieve fitness between two entities: the form in question and its context. The form is the solution to the problem; the context defines the problem." [13]

Individual builders vary their work, of course, but they do not tamper much with the form of the object. Once set in the community's traditional repertoire of ideas, a house's form—its type—remains steadfast. Traditional builders are more apt to vary the fabric, the skin, of a building, and they are even more apt to vary the structure's use over time. In conducting research, the folk-architecture specialist should look at four primary features in a building: its form, construction, use, and decoration.[14] Form, construction, and use are essential to a classification of folk buildings. *Form* refers to the floorplan (horizontal layout) and vertical organization (massing and openings). *Construction* refers to the mode and techniques used for converting the trees, boulders, and mud of nature into the fragile shelters used for the life and work of culture. *Use* refers to how the buildings are employed to meet their original and successive tasks. *Decoration* refers to the ways in which cool objects are furnished with the warmth of ornamentation.

Of the four elements, form is the most important in deciphering a structure's place in the repertory of traditional types. It is a hallmark of folk buildings that they fall into typologies (like ballads or folktales) based on form. Form changes little over time. Whether corn knives or clay pots, folk things tend to vary little over time but much over space—and the opposite is true for fashionable things and academic architecture. Within the duplication of form, however, there is room for change, because architecture, like language, changes continually. Folk builders certainly adopt fashions when they can be accommodated into their traditional areas of competence. In folk buildings, the changes occur in the variation of known forms.[15] Variation usually indicates not new types but new motifs—ornamentation, a turn of phrase in a song, a finial on a chair—and rarely the kind of variation that alters basic formal structure. Farmhouses remain folk houses despite the application of Greek revival or Gothic gingerbread touches. The bold Gothic revival did not really catch on at the folk level in Little Dixie, but as in other regions of the United States that very useful Gothic dormer was stuck on and became a familiar decorative dash on farmhouses; it represented a hint toward fashion as well as allowing for more light, ventilation, and space in the loft. In the previous century (the eighteenth), the Georgian period wrought significant changes in the form and decoration of folk houses, and the results were largely complete before Little Dixie's first effective settlement.[16] Form tends to remain stable, while construction, use, and decoration tend to vary.

The materials and techniques of construction can vary greatly, but for our purposes if the structure is built according to traditional plan and type, it is a "folk" building. A single-pen house built on a farm in Randolph County, Missouri, in 1976 may have been built by the inexpensive and efficient balloon-frame method with entirely mass-produced materials—cement-block footings, kiln-dried yellow-pine lumber from a Georgia tree farm, cheap wire nails, prefabricated rafter trusses, corrugated galvanized tin roofing, and so forth, at least partly put together with electric tools—but if that house conforms in *type* to traditional

Little Dixie single-pen houses, it is a folk building. The builder's intention was to put up a standard small house, and he naturally took advantage of modern materials and technology. This little house I've just described (probably built for a tenant family) may be a folk building of lesser purity or technical quality than its 1776 or 1876 precursor, but it is no less interesting and valuable to the student of culture. Indeed, we might find the replication of an old house type by a modern farmer extremely fascinating because of the many possible aspects of culture change and mental process that it suggests. And this discussion only glances at the roles of the builder and carpenter, roles largely unchanged and still traditional in spite of radical developments in technology. The ways in which a modern "builder" draws up contracts and plans and deals with his clients involve a complicated set of unwritten codes and customs based on generations of experience and tradition. A folk carpenter is a folk carpenter whether the ripsaw is powered by gasoline or electricity or human muscle.

As for use, usage of traditional buildings varies greatly, as I have suggested elsewhere. A change in the practical uses to which a folk building is put does not wipe out its real identification as a folk house or barn. Moreover, the same perfectly traditional building may have different uses at the same time: the structure we think of as a smokehouse only performs that task for a few weeks each winter, and the rest of the year it is a catchall storage shed.

Decoration, often ignored by folklorists and stressed too much by art historians, gives us information about the building's (and the builder's) relationship with fashion and popular turns in national taste (Figure 2–3). It is often the decoration of houses that makes them memorable or important to the people in the community, not the fine and ancient ways in which their rooms are laid out. But like floorplans, decorations also tend to become formalized. After use and reuse over years, certain decorative elements that stick (like those ornamental milled wooden brackets nailed on porches and gables) actually become a part of the character of folk houses of the time, so that by the end of the nineteenth century certain decorations had become customary on finely built farmhouses. Those fancy wooden curlicues have nothing to do with the house's type, its manner of construction, or its use when built, but they do reflect its aesthetic purpose. The overwhelming folk cultural drive for repetition and stability of form is maintained, while the personality of the individual house is enhanced by the owner's choice of trim within the available accepted pool of possibilities. Those Gothic swirls in roof corners lend added beauty. The houses are indeed artistic, but artistic "only to a degree that does not hinder their practical effect."[17]

Figure 2–3. Function and beauty are linked in this window in the back door to the kitchen in the ell of a frame central-hall I house between Mt. Airy and Salisbury, Randolph County.

Though diverse national and ethnic cultures were represented in the early settlement of America, the architectural forms brought to the historic East and South by the Spanish, French, Dutch, and Swedes generally gave away to the dominant British house plans. The basic American folk house, found in abundance across Missouri as across the nation, derives from British originals dating back hundreds of years, and that dwelling shape was combined here with German woodworking skills to produce the perfect syncretism: the American log house, ideally a square or slightly rectangular house based on the fundamental one-room English sixteen-foot-square "hall." That basic building block was set in place in Little Dixie in the early nineteenth century, as it was in Massachusetts, Virginia, and the Carolinas in the seventeenth. Scholars have invented the term *single-pen house* for that basic building block. This essential unit was endlessly repeated, and two photographs can be paired to suggest the range of transformations that the single-pen house underwent in this region of the Midwest (Figure 2–4). The ways houses are generated from rule sets in folk culture are explained in Henry Glassie's *Semiotica* article and more fully in his *Folk Housing in Middle Virginia*, where exacting diagrams represent every house type and every variant in two Virginia counties where every folk house was documented in the field.

A

Figure 2–4. The basic Anglo-American house and its ultimate transformation. A is a single-pen house in Higbee, Randolph County, with handsome and typical carpenter Gothic porch posts and trim. B is a ne plus ultra red-brick five-bay central-hall I house of the sort known as "old southern mansions," in Fulton, Callaway County.

B

Studies of material culture should begin, like any other journey of discovery and analysis, with a problem to solve or a thesis to test. Material-culture studies should involve the complete analysis of objects or clusters of objects in their physical and cultural contexts. The aim of material-culture research is the thoughtful study of groups or "profiles"

of essential ingredients. An architectural profile, then, is a combination of four important ingredients to be accounted for in field and library documentation: (1) complete artifactual description (plan, construction, use, decoration); (2) sketch maps and information on the physical setting on the land; (3) information on the building or constellation of buildings in formal history and through time from the usual primary and secondary historical sources, public records, and archival holdings; and (4) information from the vital, often enigmatic and electrifying, informal history that can be obtained through thoughtful interviews with the family, neighbors, and "county oracles" (the persons in every locale who possess and cherish unwritten, oral tradition and the subtle unofficial history of the community) who give the dimensions of life and passion to the history of old objects. A good study in situ for an architectural profile would give us the facts of form, time, and space (the what and how, the when and where), which, when joined with formal and informal historical information (the who and why), would allow us to sort out our puzzles of cultural expression and meaning. Shouldering a sheaf of field materials (packed notebook, rolls of spent film, and sound-recording tapes) and library research, the folk historian is ready to repair to a seminar room or kitchen table to catalog and seek to explain the profile of the farm or building with whatever theories and visions solve the problem at hand.[18]

Figure 2–5. Fall hunting camp in Little Dixie, 1899. Marshall family album.

3
Building Little Dixie: The Houses

Little Dixie architecture spans the history of Anglo-American folk building in the South and lower Midwest, compressing into about a hundred years some three hundred years in the development of forms and techniques of construction based on old models and intentions, ranging from America's medieval seventeenth century up to the end of the robustly complicated Victorian era of the early twentieth century. Significant chapters in the history of building in wood in central and northwestern Europe from the deeper Middle Ages forward can be read in the buildings of this area of central Missouri. In Little Dixie, there is a kind of ultimate summary of "American" traditional building, powered so much by British antecedents, as it moved west from the Mid-Atlantic, Chesapeake Tidewater and Piedmont over the Blue Ridge Mountains and through the Bluegrass to this section of Missouri bounded by two famous rivers whose creeks drain rich farm ground.

Architectural traditions here compose a narrative that is particularly midwestern and particularly nineteenth century, but also clearly rooted in earlier days and faraway places. This is a complicated region by any reckoning, and it was made more so in the nineteenth century by the conditions of this Missouri frontier and the "gateway" personality of a new state with great navigable rivers and jumping-off places for people heading into the vast plains and the Rocky Mountains beyond.

Travelers in nineteenth-century America were often struck by the regional character of everything from furniture to fiddle tunes. It is in traditional architecture, too, that people tended to put a clear stamp on the landscape hinting of old but distinctive customs.[1] It is a hallmark of folk culture that it manifests itself regionally (whether in a jammed urban neighborhood or in a deep, long desert valley) and that certain kinds of man-made artifacts—chairs, pottery, gravestones, fences, houses, and other objects carried along in the movers' wagons or minds—are extremely helpful in figuring out what makes places like Bluegrass Kentucky or Little Dixie tick.[2] Houses can and should be studied in their cultural and environmental contexts as regional signposts and as "social

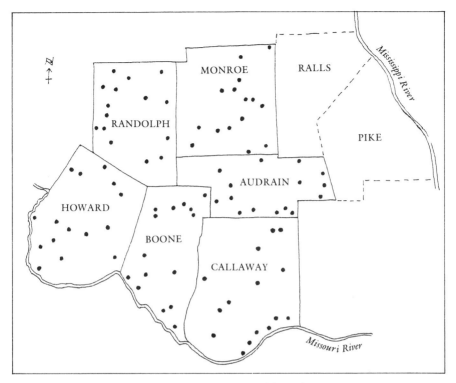

Figure 3–1. Buildings recorded in the test Little Dixie region.

documents" sending us messages about real cultural meaning not easily obtainable from formal historical records or from oral testimony.[3] Old artifacts tell us not only about their builders and users, but also about changes in their communities and their position in relation to larger patterns and moods across the nation.[4]

At the risk of repetition, floorplans are often the starting point in studying the ways rural buildings are made. Plans are vital to identifying diffusion patterns, provenience, antecedents, and other factors adding up to an understanding of regional character.[5] Though form is paramount, methods of construction, use, and decoration are also significant parts of the field documentation. In classifying building types, layout and other primary characteristics (height, massing) are used; by their stability and ease of inspection, plans of traditional buildings allow access to the heart of the structure.[6]

Plans of the basic buildings in Little Dixie indicate a pattern of two main parts. First, the architecture of old buildings here shows a meaningful similarity in type to those buildings dominant in the South where the first permanent settlers came from. Second, the architecture here has a separate personality that is the result of local forces of climate, land, materials, skills, so that the buildings here were not just mere copies of familiar structures in Virginia or Kentucky.

Many features of southern material culture inherited by Little Dixie came from Pennsylvania and the Middle Atlantic states, for example, the horizontal log construction techniques developed by Palatine Germans and spread throughout the South as they and their Scotch-Irish neighbors settled in the valley of Virginia, along the Blue Ridge Mountains, and finally into areas like the Tennessee valley and the Kentucky Bluegrass.[7] House types in Little Dixie are southern, but moreover they are Anglo-American structures with the main entrance in the long side. The main dwelling types in Little Dixie are also the main types of the South: (1) single-pen houses, (2) double-pen houses, including the hall-and-parlor and the saddlebag subtypes, (3) central-hall houses, including the dogtrot subtype, (4) stack houses, and (5) I houses.[8]

A certain barn type, the transverse crib, occurs across Little Dixie and is diagnostic of a southern architectural influence and diffusion of ideas. It occurs more frequently than any other type, including more noticeable "old" barn types like the single crib, the so-called English barn, and the double crib. The dogtrot house—actually a central-hall subtype with an open breezeway between two main rooms—and the transverse-crib barn both seem to have developed in the early nineteenth century in the lowland parts of the South's interior, particularly in the Tennessee valley, according to Glassie's reckoning.[9]

In a series of papers in the material-culture journal *Pioneer America*, Glassie explains the types and variations of double-crib barns in Pennsylvania,[10] and there are similar log double-crib barns that have survived in Little Dixie, especially along the Missouri River in Callaway and Boone counties where the barns are covered with vertical boards to protect the log walls and frame sheds have been attached to them. In Missouri, the oldest barns documented in this project were of the double-crib and single-crib varieties, built of logs. The shift to transverse-crib barns of frame construction occurred after the Civil War, when they soon replaced the old log barns. The new barns were built both of heavy timber frame using mortise-and-tenon joinery and hewn timbers and the modern balloon-frame system of nailing together sawed, lightly braced timbers.

The most telling house type in Little Dixie is the I house, which developed in lowland areas and the Kentucky Bluegrass (though it has clear antecedents in Britain) and was carried to Missouri and planted firmly as the main farmhouse of the successful settler (Figure 3–2). When German farmers took up residence in Little Dixie, they adopted "English" houses (I houses, hall-and-parlor houses, single-pen houses, central-hall houses) in order to settle into the community easily, but these Germans kept their stout, justly famous barns as the principal building on their farms here just as they did in the valley of Virginia, in southern Indiana, and in the Ozark plateau area at Little Dixie's perimeter.[11]

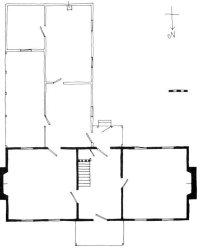

Figure 3–2. This "old southern mansion," a magnificent frame central-hall I house with Greek revival detailing between Lisbon and Boonesboro in Howard County, was converted into a hay barn years ago. The people gone, the old house functions as a visual reminder of the past as well as sheltering the farmer's hay crop inside its once-elegant facade.

Along with the dominance of southern Anglo-American houses and transverse-crib barns from the Bluegrass and the valley of Tennessee, the great wealth of fine log construction comprises the third principal factor in the Little Dixie architectural landscape that suggests its great correspondence with the home areas of the pioneer farmers. Samples from the scholarship on Kentucky folk architecture indicate the dominance there of a similar pattern of I houses, single-pen houses, saddlebag houses, and hall-and-parlor houses. Rexford Newcomb's *Old Kentucky Architecture* stresses "fine old Colonial, Georgian and Greek Revival mansions," which include many traditional I houses dressed up in the Sunday clothes of "style," and James C. Thomas has a photographic essay with photographs of Kentucky buildings that could as well be located in central Missouri. Clay Lancaster describes building in Fayette County, Kentucky, which is particularly relevant since many Missouri settlers were from there; his discussions of how log building dominated in the earliest settlement phase and then was gradually replaced by frame, of the use of brick, and of the rareness of stone construction ring true for Little Dixie. A bicentennial essay on Kentucky building also contains many examples of houses and barns like those in Little Dixie.[12]

The Building Types and Their Variations in Little Dixie

The southern hunters and farmers were not the first to settle in Missouri, but of the two streams of Spanish and French influence, only the French left much of an imprint in the Little Dixie area, and it is visible now mainly along the Mississippi River from above Hannibal south and in the inland areas southwest of St. Louis. There was a French village at Cote Sans Dessein in Callaway County, but it was swept away by flood waters.[13]

There are some similarities between Little Dixie house types and those in the Deep South and in the Arkansas Ozarks,[14] but these are insignificant and late in time. German building in central Missouri along the Missouri River, an area amounting to Little Dixie's southern edge, is documented by van Ravenswaay, and German log building in Texas has been studied by Terry Jordan, but Little Dixie architecture shows little German influence.[15]

Other House Types. Northern and New England house types are practically nonexistent in Little Dixie, but there is an occasional "T house" found in the region (Figures 3–3 through 3–5). Two-story I houses were built in the late nineteenth century, but by this time the

Figure 3–3. A two-story T house (called "yankee houses" in Little Dixie) between Hallsville and Murry, Boone County.

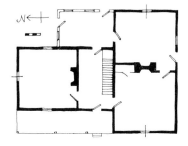

classic southern big house type (the I house) was fading in popularity and had begun to seem old-fashioned to many people. The T house hints of New England and upper Midwest influences (where the Greek revival period made a deep impression) and also suggests that carpenters' manuals and pattern books were becoming widespread in Victorian days. Pattern books like those by Calvert Vaux, Asher Benjamin, and Andrew Jackson Downing helped popularize fashionable house styles that often contained traditional room sizes and floorplans at their cores. Despite the shifting of the "front" of the house to place the tall gable to the road, the interior spaces and room arrangements were comfortable to southerners and northerners alike.[16] There are T houses with similar wings that represent the smaller and more usual version of these pattern-book-influenced folk houses. The late, small dwellings occur widely across the Midwest and upland South, and they are built in communities that took the T-house form into the repertoire of tradition. Though it comes from popular trends and plan books of the day, it was built and

A

Figure 3–4. One-story T houses in Little Dixie. A is between Hallsville and Centralia in Boone County. B is between Moberly and Madison in Randolph County. Both are built of balloon-frame construction, have porches front and rear, and similar set of rooms. It is clear that more expense was paid to applying ornamentation from the lumberyard to the Boone County house.

B

used by "traditional" people, accepted in the late nineteenth century (when many parts of community life were changing), and should be documented and studied along with the more recognized and older folk-house types. Its touches of fashion and influence from academic architecture make it more, not less, fascinating in its living context in the countryside. L-shaped, one-story T houses are especially abundant in towns and remind us of the interesting ways people incorporate fashion into folk culture. The houses are painted, decorated, and furnished in the same way and suggest the tendency to adopt new designs when they fit in with the prevailing community view of things. In our long continuum of architecture, these houses fall somewhere between the firmly "folk" house types (like single-pen and I houses) and the nonfolk or academic houses at the other end of the line.

Figure 3–5. This "modern house" may be seen as an elaborate T house. It was built in 1891–1892 by Dudley T. Bradley between Huntsville and Higbee in Randolph County. Bradley's great-great-grandfather Terry Thomas Bradley emigrated from Northern Ireland to Piedmont North Carolina in 1750; his son Leonard served in the Revolution and came to Missouri around 1830; his son Terry established the major farm operation; his son William T. was a Gold Rush forty-niner who died in Hangtown, California; his son was Dudley T. Bradley, the house's builder and a farmer of exceptional success. After several years of standing vacant, the house was restored by W. L. and Dorothy Ann Bradley Robb around 1978.

There are many fine large farmhouses throughout Little Dixie that are the result of popular designs of the late nineteenth century but that, like the T house, were built and used in the same way as "folk" houses. These big frame houses generally became the replacement for the great old southern I houses—just as the one-story T house generally replaced smaller and older folk-house types. These big farmhouses, like the Bradley place (Figure 3–5), have begun to be gradually and steadily replaced by even more modern red-brick one-story "ramblers" or ranch-style houses of contemporary popular design. Houses like the Bradley place are in effect the first of the large Little Dixie farmhouses that really seem "modern" to our eyes. They are found both in town and in the country and, although they were built to individual specifications according to different floorplans, they seem to have been based on only a few general room orientations. They have no particular "type" or category in the regular architectural record and may be seen separately or as a nicely complicated variant of the two-story T-house type established in the region earlier. Many farmers in Little Dixie, as everywhere, built small dwellings to their own design that satisfied the needs and wants of their families. Like Earl Westfall's house (Figure 3–6), they seem to be part of no old established category of folk houses, but stand on their own somewhere in the gray zones between "folk" and "academic" architecture.

Figure 3–6. Basketmaker and farmer Earl Westfall conceived of the layout and design of his home near Higbee, Howard County, by sitting under a tree and sizing up the building site and his own family's needs in 1947; the four-room house faintly echoes the so-called bungalows that were built in town in the early twentieth century.

Folk Houses in Little Dixie

Architecture's Building Block: The Single-Pen House. The single-pen house, either square or slightly rectangular and often called a "cabin," has a plan of one room and is either one or one and a half stories high (Figure 3–7). Its usual dimensions, as in Virginia and Kentucky, are about 16 feet by 16 feet, 16 by 18, or 16 by 22.[17] Like other houses, these little dwellings are set off the ground on piers at the corners. I recorded eighteen single-pen houses in Little Dixie—in the original six "test" counties in 1974, though most of the examples occurred in Boone and Howard counties[18]—and eleven were rectangular rather than the square shape more customary in the Virginia Tidewater. By the time the single-pen form got to the Bluegrass (and to Missouri), the rectangular mode had become the standard. Most of the single-pen houses I found had been altered by the addition of one or more rooms, usually in a frame shed addition on the rear or in another building block added to one gable end (resulting in a double-pen house). There are still many fine log single-pen houses surviving from the early settlement period; seventeen of the eighteen houses of this type I recorded were built of

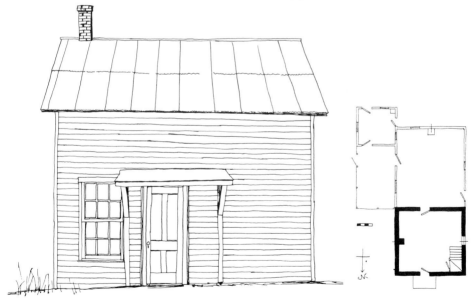

Figure 3–7. "The old John Wells place" is a V-notched log single-pen house covered with the customary lapped weatherboarding, painted white; it measures 15′1″ × 17′5″ and has a sleeping loft and frame room additions on the rear. It was built on Bachelor Creek between Bachelor and Calwood in Callaway County by a Kentucky farmer in about 1832, and it faces north to the road.

logs, and most of these dated from the first period. The V-notching method of joining the corners is the customary mode for single-pen houses; larger house types sometimes are V-notched, but these may be notched in other ways, too. Fifteen of the seventeen log houses I examined were V-notched, and most were covered with horizontal lapped weatherboarding; this does not imply that V-notching is at the bottom of some imaginary scale of evolution for log construction methods, only that V-notching was the main technique known to the settlers.

None of the very earliest and temporary log "cabins" has lasted for us to examine. There are fascinating drawings of these in travelers' accounts and other early publications, and various writers tried to describe them. These early shelters were single-pen houses constructed in a primitive manner, built with unbarked round logs, with cat-and-clay chimneys, puncheon floors, and leaky roofs of loosely rived boards or long shakes held down with weighted poles (Figure 3–8).[19]

Transformations of the Single-Pen House. The single-pen house is the basic Anglo-American dwelling form in Little Dixie, as it is across the regions from which the area was settled. The changes people make to these "cabins" when enlarging them indicate particular rules for deal-

Figure 3–8. Early "log cabin." Round-log cabin, ca. 1820, from *Missouri, A Guide to the Show-Me State*, compiled by the Federal Writers' Project in 1941.

ing with living space based on generations of experimentation and gradual satisfaction through successful solutions to the problem. There are three ways to acquire more space in a one-room dwelling, two of which are very limited, and the third of which is potentially endless: (1) inside, (2) upward, and (3) sideways or rearward (Figures 3–9 through 3–12). All three methods of enlargement can be found in the same structure. First, in a subtractive interior division, the basic one-room rectangle or square is divided by a light frame partition into two smaller rooms, customarily a kitchen and a living area. Since single-pen houses in Little Dixie usually have a sleeping loft under the roof, this actually yields three separate, if cramped, rooms. Lofts were unheated and intended only for sleeping and storage. The dwelling that results from this type of division, a subtype of the double-pen house, is the hall-and-parlor house (Figure 3–9C$_1$). Next, the one-room house can be doubled upward, making a stack house (Figure 3–9A). Next, there is the most common expansion method, the addition of a room or rooms to one gable end, creating a double-pen house (Figure 3–9C$_2$ and C$_3$). A central-hall house results when the second basic building block is placed in line with the first, but separated by a hallway (Figure 3–9D$_1$ and D$_2$). When double-pen houses and central-hall houses are expanded through the addition of a full second story, I houses result (Figure 3–9B$_1$, B$_2$, and B$_3$). In one case,

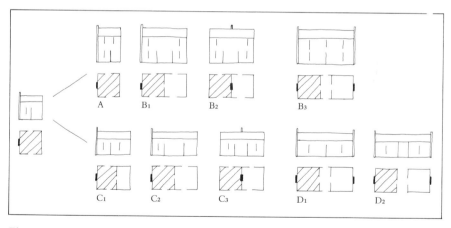

Figure 3–9. Traditional Little Dixie houses built by southerners in the nineteenth century. All these are transformations of the single-pen house at left. A is a stack house. B$_1$, a basic I house. B$_2$, a saddlebag subtype of the I house. B$_3$, a central-hall I house. C$_1$, a hall-and-parlor subtype of the double-pen house. C$_2$, a double-pen house. C$_3$, a saddlebag subtype of the double-pen house. D$_1$, a central-hall house. D$_2$, a dogtrot subtype of the central-hall house. This simple diagram traces the career of the single-pen house as the basic building block in Little Dixie architecture but does not show evolution. All these houses existed in the eastern and southern source areas and did not develop in Missouri.

the Kivett log house (Figure 3–13), two full rooms were added beyond the east gable wall, set off by a tiny frame storeroom, resulting in a simple lateral enlargement of the double-pen house type. In the fanciest version of a single-pen house growing larger, the old Todd house (Figure 3–14) on Doe Creek in Howard County was expanded in at least two distinct phases. Initially, a hallway, a loft entrance, and a large balanced room were added to the basic frame dwelling, and then two long rooms were added as a shed addition to the rear. The final additions by the Todd family enlarged the house so that it now suggests the standard first-rate

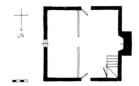

Figure 3–10. A light frame partition made the Sapping-ton house, a V-notched log single-pen house measuring about 17′ × 18′, functionally a two-room hall-and-par-lor house. There is a sleeping loft, too; the house is on Hungry Mother Creek near Bunker Hill, Howard County.

Figure 3–11. "The old Martin place" on Sandy Creek between Gazette and Mt. Carmel in Audrain County was built by John A. Martin, from Kentucky, in 1850, and is a V-notched log single-pen house (15′ × 17′) with a loft and frame shed addition on the rear. The log bearing walls were covered with weatherboarding early, then in the 1950s covered again with brown "brick" asbestos siding at the same time the corrugated tin sheets were nailed over the old rived-shingle roof. The original red brick "English" chim-ney stands and was converted to a stove flue. The interior bare log walls are smoothly chinked and whitewashed. The little house is used now as a storage shed and faces south. As in many log houses, there is a tiny cupboard built into the front wall.

Figure 3–12. This V-notched log single-pen house once had a large exterior stone chimney. Located between Riggs and Sturgeon in Boone County, it now serves as a granary. In form and construction, it is typical of most early log houses—it has a boxed-in stairway, its interior walls are carefully chinked but the bare logs were not covered (they were whitewashed), its doors are directly opposite each other, it has a gable roof, its outside walls were covered with horizontal siding soon after construction, and it measures about 18 by 20 feet.

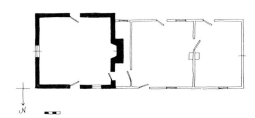

Figure 3–13. The half-dovetailed log single-pen house on the Kivett farm near Boonesboro in Howard County was built by an ancestor of Mr. Clifton Kivett who came from Virginia in 1840. The interior walls of the log house are whitewashed, it measures 16′7″ × 18′8″, and the enlarged building is sided. The original chimney of limestone still functions.

Figure 3–14. "The old Todd place" between Harrisburg and Fayette was built about 1845, with later frame additions. The original frame house measures 15′3″ × 16′5″ and has a full brick exterior chimney. The Todds came from Virginia.

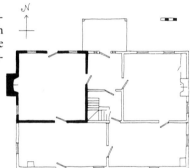

two-story house type in the region, the I house. Finally, a house can be enlarged through the addition of rooms on the rear wall, as in the John Wells house in Callaway County. Such rearward extensions ("sheds" or "ells" or "T's" in shape) are usually graced by a side porch and often have an extra smaller room or two tacked on later. In houses like the Wells place, the original log single-pen house (sided at the time of construction) becomes a sort of living room, and the new frame addition on the rear becomes the kitchen.

It is clear that the humble "log cabins" of the first settlers were stout and durable and designed to be maintained and added to as time, resources, and a growing family permitted. These were certainly not rude temporary shelters, as many writers want us to believe. Throughout the classic architectural regions of America, additions are easily made to basic one-room houses (Figures 3–15 and 3–16). In addition, most of the

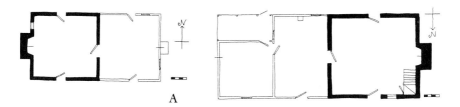

A

B

Figure 3–15. Lateral additions to single-pen houses. A is a 15′1″ × 16′9″ V-notched log house with frame room addition built by Kentucky emigrant Ezekial Bryan in 1857, on Turkey Creek south of Paris, Monroe County. B is a 18′10″ × 21′1″ V-notched log house with added rooms and porch built by Virginia emigrant Logan Lee about 1840, on Batts Creek between Glasgow and Roanoke in Howard County. C is "the old Swetnam place," a 16′ × 18′ V-notched log house with added frame rooms built about 1840 between Darksville and Grand Center, Randolph County. D is the old McKinney place west of St. Martins in Cole County, at the southern edge of Little Dixie's zone of transition; the Virginia emigrant built a 16′8″ × 16′9″ V-notched story-and-a-half-tall single-pen house and added several framed rooms and an attached summer kitchen on the rear.

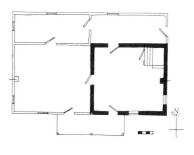

C

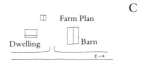

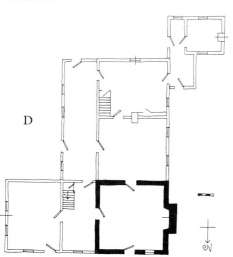

D

Figure 3–16. In a rare method of extension, this single-pen house in Millersburg, Callaway County, was added to with a narrow ell on the rear. Ell additions are common on larger house types, but unusual on small ones.

larger house types that the expanded single-pen houses develop into were commonly known in Europe, so enlargements of small dwellings do not indicate an evolution in architectural forms in this country.[20] Further, two- and three-bay houses were the norm in Virginia as well as in England, and it is probable that many builders of single-pen houses in Missouri fully intended to enlarge them from the very beginning. Temporary poverty or the necessities of work may have prevented some settlers from erecting double-pen or other house types at first, but it is important to remember the broad currency and availability of all the standard Little Dixie folk-house types in the eastern source areas. For many farmers, building a tidy single-pen house was the logical first phase in the sometimes lengthy process of arriving at a completely suitable house. They merely selected the obvious basic building block and began with it, knowing it could be added to when conditions permitted. This is the process of folk architecture, a process in which people cope with the problems of getting a fresh start in a new land and of expanding spatial needs—a process that operates in very particular ways grounded in cultural history, habit, function, and community tradition.

The Block Repeated: The Double-Pen House. The double-pen house is composed of two basic units of roughly the same size and proportions arranged laterally (Figures 3–17 through 3–26). It is basically two

Figure 3–17. A double-pen house (hall-and-parlor subtype) in Audrain County.

single-pen houses built side by side. As an extension of the single-pen house, it is similar in its spatial arrangement, openings, roof construction, and other technical aspects. As we have seen, single-pen houses get added on to in ways that make the resulting facade look like a double pen; but upon close examination these houses turn out to be altered single-pen houses and not originally built as a double-pen. As with other basically southern as well as British folk houses, the main entrance of a double-pen house is located on the long side (not in the gable) facing

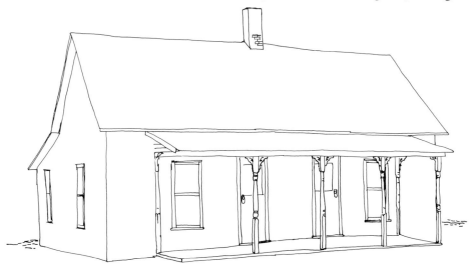

Figure 3–18. A double-pen house (saddlebag subtype) in Browns Station, Boone County.

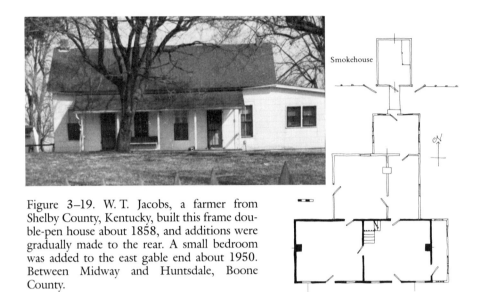

Figure 3–19. W. T. Jacobs, a farmer from Shelby County, Kentucky, built this frame double-pen house about 1858, and additions were gradually made to the rear. A small bedroom was added to the east gable end about 1950. Between Midway and Huntsdale, Boone County.

outward to the road or street. In Little Dixie, double pens occur in three basic forms: the essential double-pen house, the hall-and-parlor house, and the saddlebag house. The plain double pen is the oldest sort in Little Dixie, but it is rarer now than the other two subtypes; it is composed of two single rooms built with chimneys in the gable ends. The placement of the chimney is decisive in separating the various double-pen houses into subtypes. The hall-and-parlor house, an important dwelling type in sixteenth- and seventeenth-century Britain, is also a distinctive type in the Virginia and Carolina Tidewater and Piedmont source areas and across the Blue Ridge Mountains in central Kentucky. It is composed of two unequal rooms, and the significant exterior feature is its single front door. Chimneys or stove flues may be placed in the gables or in the middle of the house. In log examples, the two rooms are parted by a frame partition, often of wide vertical boards. The Penn-Clemens house in Monroe County is a famous hall-and-parlor house due to an accident of birth: Samuel Clemens was born there. It was built by a Tennessee emigrant, William N. Penn, in 1834 and was recently moved to the Mark Twain State Park, where it is now the Mark Twain Memorial Shrine maintained by the State of Missouri (Figure 3–24).

The third subtype is the saddlebag house, distinguished by its two front doors and central chimney. Saddlebag houses are nearly always built with a simple balloon frame and are widely distributed across the lower Midwest beyond Little Dixie. The two rooms of the saddlebag

Figure 3–20. Almost tumbled in, this V-notched log double-pen house retains its original six-light double-hung windows and original weatherboarding. It is located near Williamsburg in Callaway County and was built around 1850.

house are warmed by the same fireplace or stove flue. Originally built with large stone chimneys with hearths serving both rooms, and built now with brick stove flues and stove holes, the saddlebag house is marked by the efficient placement of its chimneys.

In Little Dixie, double-pen houses were sometimes built of V-notched logs, but usually they were built of frame and sided with lapped horizontal weatherboarding. They are one or one and a half stories high and traditionally added onto at the rear. Early examples of plain double-pen houses are sometimes constructed irregularly, as in the Marion Lee house in Howard County. As with other traditional folk-house types, the later these houses were built, and the more their pattern had become fixed in the community's set of customary architectural rules, the more rigorously symmetrical the houses became.

Figure 3–21. The rooms of this frame double-pen house measure 17′ × 17′4″ and 15′3″ × 15′3″ and thus do not match. The builder, Virginia settler Marion Lee, added a summer kitchen across a small hallway on the rear of the house. In the "Chariton community" between Glasgow and Roanoke in Howard County, the house was built about 1845.

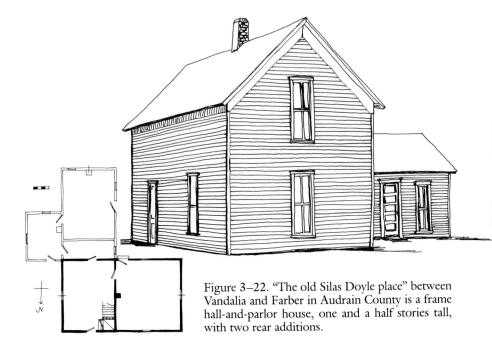

Figure 3–22. "The old Silas Doyle place" between Vandalia and Farber in Audrain County is a frame hall-and-parlor house, one and a half stories tall, with two rear additions.

Figure 3–23. The well-known Missouri painter George Caleb Bingham built this house in Arrow Rock (in Little Dixie's zone of transition in Saline County) in 1837; it is a brick hall-and-parlor folk house. Photograph by Hadley K. Irwin. Courtesy of the Division of Parks and Historic Preservation, Missouri Department of Natural Resources.

Figure 3–24. When the Penn-Clemens house (where Mark Twain was born in 1835) was restored and moved to Mark Twain State Park, it lost its front porch, its rear addition, and its physical context—and much of its character. The house is shown here stripped of its additions, just before it was moved. Photograph courtesy of the Division of Parks and Historic Preservation, Missouri Department of Natural Resources.

Figure 3–25. In this frame saddlebag house near Youngs Creek between Thompson and Rowena in Audrain County, the two rooms are almost exactly 15′ × 15′2″. It was built around 1915.

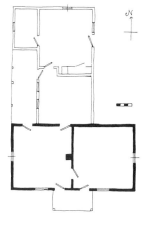

Figure 3–26. The "old Moses Payne place" on the Missouri River bluffs between Rocheport and Huntsdale in Howard County is a famous local landmark, but the house people remark upon—a huge white frame central-hall I house—was added to the original dwelling, a heavy frame saddlebag house with an immense stone central chimney. The walls of the original saddlebag house (which to modern eyes looks like an "addition" to the big fancy I house) are filled in with brick nogging in half-timber fashion. As with many Little Dixie chimneys, the flue top is made of brick. The hand-hewn timbers and brick infill in the original building are hidden to casual observers by the weatherboarding. This is a nice example of an addition to an old house completely altering people's perception of the dwelling type.

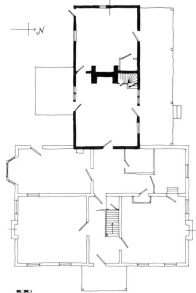

Adding a Formal Middle: The Central-Hall House. The central-hall house type includes houses of one or one and a half stories that have a basic two-room plan, but with a central hallway balanced between the two rooms (Figures 3–27 through 3–33). The central-hall house category also includes what are known as "dogtrot" houses. Central-hall houses may have rear ell or shed additions and small front porches. They occur in log (almost always sided with horizontal weatherboarding), frame, brick, and half-timbering construction, and like other folk houses in Little Dixie, most are log or frame. Five of the seventeen central-hall houses I documented during the field research were of the dogtrot sub-type. Many central-hall houses are in the classic folk form dressed up handsomely with Greek revival or Gothic ornamentation; some combine architectural details of several different periods or styles. Indeed, some of these (like some I houses) combine in their appearance three main "styles" found on folk buildings from the late eighteenth and nineteenth centuries: a solid, balanced, orderly symmetry of bays and openings reflecting Georgian period influences, Greek revival cornices (fenestration with dentils and boxed gables), and this topped off with the later addition to the same house of a Gothic revival gable centered over the front door and porch. The separate central hall itself came firmly into traditional architecture as a result of the influential Georgian period.

The term *dogtrot house* is known widely across the lower Midwest and South, but there is confusion over what exactly constitutes the type and disagreement about the dwelling's particular European origins (whether it is a northwest European or essentially a southern American form). Log dogtrot houses are certainly easy to spot if in their original shape: there are two log pens with doors opening into a breezeway under a common roof. They are one-story houses essentially, but often have sleeping lofts under the roof. The broad open hallway or breezeway—the "dogtrot"—is the hallmark of the dogtrot house, but most breezeways were eventually enclosed when the log house was sided and the breezeway was converted into a central hall inside the house.[21] If this hallway was wide and open originally—regardless of whether the building is frame or log—the house is a dogtrot house. There are some dogtrot houses today in Little Dixie that seem from the outside to be simple central-hall houses and not dogtrots. And most houses in the Midwest that look like frame dogtrots are really central-hall houses, as upon close examination it can be seen that their hallways were never open.

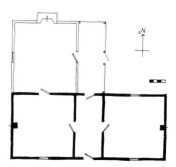

Figure 3–27. Frame central-hall house on Bonne Femme Creek between Burton and Bunker Hill in Howard County. Its main rooms measure 15′3″ × 15′4″ and 15′3″ × 15′6″, and the kitchen ell addition has a full brick cooking fireplace. There is no sleeping loft, a rarity in Little Dixie. It now serves as a chicken house.

Figure 3–28. This frame dogtrot house between Molino and Santa Fe in Audrain
County, on the South Fork of the Salt
River, has rooms measuring 17′ × 15′ and
a breezeway measuring 10′ wide. The
breezeway or hallway was framed in some
years after construction (about 1845) and
shed rooms were added to the back of the
house. There is no sleeping loft, and this
house suggests settler-builders from hot,
lowland, or Tidewater parts of Virginia or
Kentucky. Those wide-open breezeways were
not so necessary in central Missouri, and the
winters in Missouri are surely harsher than
those where the settlers who built this house
came from.

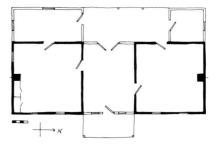

Figure 3–29. A fine specimen of the earliest central-hall houses in Little Dixie, this frame
one was built in the Missouri River bottoms near Hartsburg in Boone County in about
1830. Like other folk houses, it had a fashionable Gothic revival gable and porch tacked
on later in the nineteenth century.

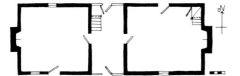

Figure 3–30. "The old Ben Roberts place" near "dead man holler" between Darksville and Jacksonville, Randolph County, is a half-dovetailed one and a half story dogtrot version of a central-hall house. Its 8'2" central hallway was originally open. The builder came from Virginia around 1850 and built not only a familiar house type but magnificent brick end chimneys characteristic of the Piedmont.

Figure 3–31. "The old George place" in Florida, Monroe County, is a square-notched log dogtrot house built by Kentuckian Robert George in about 1832. A second story was added later when the breezeway was framed in and the ell addition was put on the rear. Its rooms are 14' × 17' and 17'1", and the house was being restored when I visited the site; the siding and additions had been torn off revealing construction details and opening the old logs to the weather.

Here is an example of the early accounts of dogtrot houses in Missouri that helped establish the wide knowledge of the dwelling type:

> The dwellings of the people who emigrated from Virginia, or any of the more southern states, have usually the form of double cabins, or two distinct houses, each containing a single room, and connected to each other by a roof; the intermediate space, which is often equal in area to one of the cabins, being left open at the sides, and having the naked earth for a floor, affords a cool place and airy retreat. . . . The roof is composed of from three to five logs, laid longitudinally, and extending from end to end of the building; on these are laid the shingles, four or five feet in length; over these are three or four heavy logs, called weight poles, secured at their ends by withes, and by their weight supplying the place of nails.[22]

All of the dogtrot houses I documented in Little Dixie—in fact, all that I saw—have had their breezeways framed in and are sided with horizontal weatherboarding. These were sometimes called "double houses" by the people I visited. In *Huckleberry Finn*, Mark Twain described log houses and culture in Little Dixie, particularly in Monroe County and the vicinity of Florida, his hometown. Twain vividly described local life of the 1830s and 1840s and wrote of the Grangerford house—a dogtrot house—this way: "It was a double house, and a big open place betwixt them was roofed and floored, and sometimes the table was set there in the middle of the day, and it was a cool, comfortable place."[23]

There are many frame and log houses with central hallways that are one and a half stories high, but most of these I have arbitrarily grouped with another house type, the I house (Figure 3–34). These dwellings conform in all respects except precise height to our understanding of the

Figure 3–32. The Allen Mayo log dogtrot house (half-dovetailed, with every scrap of wood black walnut) was and is a famous landmark for local historians and citizens of Randolph County. Built in 1832 near Silver Creek west of Mt. Airy, legend says that it is the oldest house in the county still standing. It originally had full brick exterior chimneys and was covered with weatherboarding at the time of completion. Mayo is said to have been one of the county's first settlers. The Huntsville Historical Society recently moved one of the original log rooms to the town square in Huntsville and restored it— minus the original siding and the second and critical room. Future visitors will mistake the house for a single-pen "old pioneer cabin" rather than the magnificently detailed and finished log dogtrot house. It was indeed a magnificent house when I documented it in 1974.

"I house" as a folk-house type (following Kniffen's and Glassie's influential typologies) and should be considered as vertically incomplete I houses and not merely tall cabins.

An Impression of Stature: The Stack House. The stack house is made up of two proportionately equal square or slightly rectangular blocks simply stacked one on top of the other (Figures 3–35 through 3–39). This presents an impressive and tall facade to the road and provides a full second story, and there is often an attic or loft above the second floor. In terms of typology in folk architecture, before this study was done, the stack house could be thought of in two ways: as a twice as tall single-pen house,[24] or as an incomplete I house (just one room wide

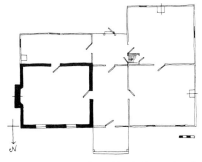

Figure 3–33. "The old Bledsoe place" in the Missouri River bottoms near Hartsburg, Boone County, was another fine log dogtrot house. The remaining log room, the east pen, is square-notched. After the west pen burned around the turn of the century, a frame room of the exact same shape was built to replace it in 1917, and the whole house was weatherboarded—creating what from the road seems to be the same original house. Here, the farmer-owner really did "restore" the house without planning to do so, and the result, now standing behind a newer brick pattern-book house, preserves the spirit of the old log dogtrot dwelling and proves the rigor of the folk tradition.

instead of two or more). Visually, the stack house suggests both house types, but the form is important enough to find its own category. For the builders and users of this sort of dwelling, who do not bother about particular names for their houses or about the scholars' awkward typologies, it falls within a general class of large farmhouses and is more like an I house than like a cabin. As a partially realized I house, the stack house can be considered as one-third of a full central-hall I house (the ultimate Little Dixie farmer's home of the nineteenth century), and two stack houses built side by side as one result in an ordinary two-room-wide I house. In one fine case in Callaway County, a central-hall I house resulted when frame stacked rooms were added onto a V-notched log stack house. The full two-story, rather narrow, balanced facade of the stack house makes it stand out from lesser neighboring houses. Most houses of this type, perhaps due to their obvious divergence in appear-

Figure 3–34. "The old Semon place" on Callahan Creek between Wood-landville and Midway in Boone County is a handsome example of a central-hall house that belongs in the I-house category. There is a forty-one-inch-wide "funeral door" in the front allowing burial caskets to be brought into the parlor for "visitation." Black slaves lived in the room above the kitchen ell addition.

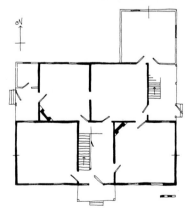

Figure 3–35. The Little Dixie stack house. "The old Jake Straw place" north of Tebbetts in Callaway County was a V-notched log stack house covered by typical weatherboarding and painted white. There was no large chimney or fireplace; a brick stove flue was located inside the south gable wall and served both floors. When I rechecked some folk houses in Callaway County in 1979, I found this grand Little Dixie house to have been demolished.

Figure 3–36. Stack houses work well in town landscapes, where building lots may be narrower than on farms; this house is at the edge of Tebbetts in Callaway County.

ance, are now greatly altered or fallen into disuse or decay. Moreover, there probably never were a great many stack houses built in Little Dixie. Most are now in Callaway County, and most were altered by various additions. Stack houses seem to have been built often by early migrants of English stock from Tidewater Maryland and Virginia or central Kentucky who settled in the gentle hills along the Missouri River. Stack houses are less common in the central and northern parts of Little Dixie. In the Chesapeake Tidewater, there are numerous stack houses, and there are many in old towns that are distinctly urban, like Alexandria, Virginia, and Annapolis, Maryland. Because of the tall and impressive yet relatively narrow facade, stack houses were well suited to urban as well as to rural landscapes. In a cramped town lot, one could build a stack house easier than its broader ideal, the I house, and research might well show the stack house to have flourished in towns more than in the country.

The doorways of these houses are always roughly centered. There is just one chimney on the main structure, though there can be additional

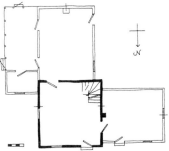

Figure 3–37. "The old Baldwin place" near Dixie between New Bloomfield and Liberty in Callaway County is a frame stack house now used as a retreat for a church group; the middle section is the original stack house.

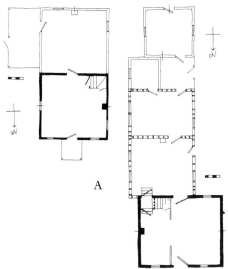

Figure 3–38. The usual mode of addition to stack houses is by placing more rooms on the rear wall. A is "the old Wells place," a frame stack house between Boonesboro and Glasgow in Howard County. B, "the old Jim Reynolds place" southeast of Madison, Monroe County, is of half-timbered construction with brick nogging for insulation; a frame smokehouse was attached to the far end of the house.

stove chimneys on kitchen additions, and this main chimney is centered in one gable end, usually the gable "to the weather" (north) if the house faces east or west. Chimneys may be inside or outside the gable wall and may serve large stone fireplaces or cast-iron woodstoves. The roofs are always pitched. If it is a log stack house, and sided, the siding is typically lapped horizontally. Entrance to the second story is via a boxed-in stairway with a little closet underneath or, less commonly, via an open stairway in a corner of the main room. Rear frame additions are common and may be either ell or shed in plan. Front porches are rare, though there is often a small unsupported pent (shed) roof over the front door for protection from the weather. Rectangular stack houses may be divided into two small rooms on the ground floor or the second floor or both by a light frame partition. I recorded nine stack houses, six of log construction (four were V-notched, two were square-notched), two of frame construction, and one of half-timber construction with brick nogging that chiefly served as insulation. Sample inside dimensions, exclud-

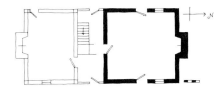

Figure 3–39. This V-notched log stack house was made into a central-hall I house through the addition of a V-notched one-and-a-half-story single-pen house across a hallway. It is located between Toledo and Yucatan on Auxvasse Creek, Callaway County.

ing additions, are 16′5″ × 15′ (V-notched, log), 15′6″ × 15′8″ (frame), 17′5″ × 15′1″ (V-notched, log) and 14′4″ × 14′2″ (V-notched, log). Stack houses are an important ingredient in the particular architectural mix that gives Little Dixie its regional flavor.

The Farmer's Mansion: The I House. This distinctive house type dominates the Little Dixie landscape, as it does the Virginia and Carolina Piedmont and the Kentucky Bluegrass. It represents the fine houses built by prosperous and ambitious farmers, some of whom were slaveholders.[25] The I house type is one room deep, two rooms in length, and two stories high (Figures 3–40 and 3–41). Early examples have tall outside end chimneys in the gables, and more recent ones have small brick chimneys for stoves. Nearly every I house has some sort of rear addition, in Little Dixie characteristically a one- or two-story ell in which the kitchen is located. The small stove flues are often dressed up with false fireplace mantelpieces or fancy shelves behind the spot where the stove sits. The minimal I house is simply a full two-story double-pen house, but the ultimate subtype—the central-hall variant—is clearly well beyond its modest kinsmen. The settlers and builders carried recollections and men-

Figure 3–40. The climax Little Dixie farmhouse, near Centralia, Boone County. A good I house must do what good poetry does—trigger the right response in the viewer/reader in order to be successful.

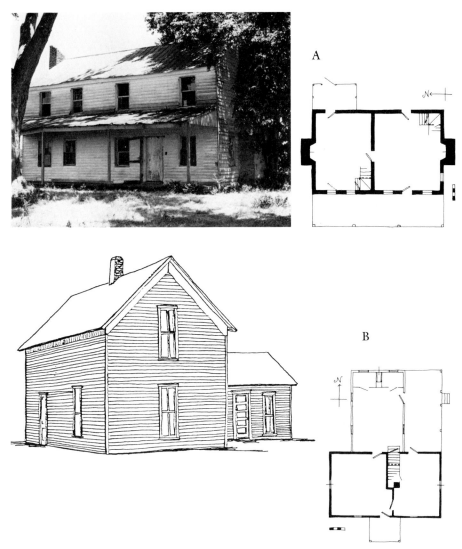

Figure 3–41. Plans of these two I houses indicate the basic two-room design. A is a half-dovetailed log I house (with two front doors) of especially fine quality on Sulphur Creek between Boonesboro and Fayette, Howard County. Each of the rooms (17′4″ × 14′9″ and 17′4″ × 17′) has a boxed-in staircase to the second floor; the house is white-washed inside and out, has stone and brick chimneys, and is weatherboarded. As in other early examples (ca. 1830), the rooms are imperfectly balanced in size. B is "the old Ogden place" on the Cuivre River between Rice's Corner and Middleton in Audrain County and is typical of later, frame two-room I houses with interior brick stove chimneys; it is a "saddlebag" subtype of the I house. The central door is almost exactly in the middle of an almost perfectly balanced 32-foot facade. The rooms are 15′5″ × 15′2″ and 15′5″ × 12′; the second room is smaller because space was stolen from it for the stairway to the second floor. Though the whole house was built at once, the darkened front portion indicates its "type" classification.

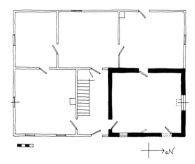

Figure 3–42. "The old Knight place," near Dixie, between New Bloomfield and Liberty in Callaway County.

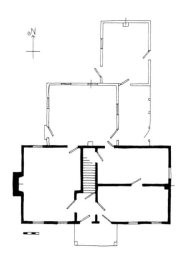

Figure 3–43. The Abraham Levick house, on Mud Creek, Levick's Mill community, Randolph County; there are two front doors and a full two-story portico.

tal plans for all kinds of folk-house types, and I houses were built very early on; they were not built just by a later and more prosperous generation. Many of the farmers coming from the Piedmont and Bluegrass areas of Virginia and Kentucky had been successful there and were able to erect fine I houses as their first dwellings in Missouri. Rather than build and use a temporary house, settlers like James F. R. Wight from Kentucky preferred to make do with canvas-wall tents pitched against mover wagons until a proper house—an I house—could be finished.[26] I houses, as we have seen, could be constructed in stages. What seems today to be a rather customary central-hall I house, the "old Knight place" near Dixie in Callaway County (Figure 3–42), began its career as a V-notched log stack house, 14′10″ × 16′9″. Some years after its construction, probably in the 1850s, frame additions were made all around—a central hallway and a balancing room to the side and then a shed addition against the new rear. The original door to the old log stack house was made into a window, and the whole structure was covered with new, white horizontal weatherboarding.

Several variations could be made to the basic I house plan, to suit personal desires for more space, more rooms, or a certain preference for the location of the chimney. An English emigrant miller, Abraham Levick, built a finely finished frame I house with a small central entrance in Randolph County in about 1845, then divided the original parlor in

Figure 3–44. The plan of the old Vandeventer place in Monroe County is more Continental and Germanic than what is typical in Little Dixie.

two to create more living and sleeping space (Figure 3–43). There is no hint of the "extra room" from outside the house. A subtype of the I house that is common in New England but very rare in Little Dixie is the central-chimney or saddlebag house. In the "old Vandeventer place" (Figure 3–44) between Florida and Perry in Monroe County, there is a massive, beautifully made central chimney of carefully shaped limestone with hearths serving both main rooms of the house. This is a curious dwelling, for the west room is made of hewn logs joined by the half-dovetailing method, while the east room is made of logs with V-notched corners. Further, each room has its own boxed-in stairway to the second story. The second story is of half-timbered construction with brick nogging between the vertical wall studs, and the half-timbering begins three logs above the ceiling joists of the first floor; the house may have started out as a one-and-a-half-story house that was later added to in height. There were several later frame additions made to the original log house, which have been stripped away. The structure now serves as a storage shed for miscellaneous farm equipment. Though a case can be made for the practical function of the central chimney—it makes for a warmer home—the ultimate source for this placement of the hearth seems to be Eastern England, where center chimney location was the accepted tradition. The central chimney is found throughout New England, which was settled primarily by emigrants from the eastern areas of England. On the other hand, most settlers coming to the Chesapeake Tidewater were from western England, where the standard traditions placed chimneys in the gable ends of houses.[27] Through our modern eyes, it is easy to account for chimney placement by environmental factors—in New England it is colder and snowier than it is in the Upland South, where outside or flush gable end chimneys have always been dominant. The effects of regional environments and weather conditions certainly fortify such traditions as hearth placement, when those traditions are logical.

The rarest subtype in the countryside is the two-thirds I house (Figure 3–45). Like the stack house, the two-thirds I house is well suited to urban landscapes and is more often found there than in the countryside. It is simply an incompleted central-hall I house, but it is an established and recurrent form and a definite subtype. Like the central-hall I house,

Figure 3–45. "The old Moss place," a two-thirds I house east of the Woodland community in Marion County in Little Dixie's zone of transition. This is a V-notched log house built by Virginia emigrants in about 1845.

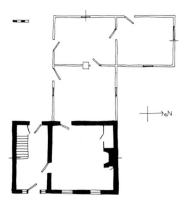

it shows the influence of the post-Renaissance urge for order propelled by the designs and thoughts of the Georgian period, when houses were squared away and made rigorously symmetrical. The two-thirds I house is made up of a broad central hall plus one of the expected two flanking rooms. From the front, it resembles standard urban Georgian side-hall houses that are two rooms deep. Most of the two-thirds I houses I encountered in Little Dixie were located in towns like Hannibal, Paris, and Glasgow.

Of the several variants of the I house I studied in this region, the most common and significant is the central-hall subtype, commonly with an ell addition on the rear. This central-hall I house form, five bays in width, is the ideal Little Dixie farmhouse of the nineteenth century. It symbolizes the aspirations of southern farmers and settlers during the period when the "Little Dixie" feeling was developing, and today it is a tangible reminder of the old ways. These houses are now thought of as "old southern mansions" by many people, and they do mirror the so-called golden age that many people think existed (but that did not in the romantic sense) in some far-off good old days.[28] They reflect the culture of memory that local historians sometimes dwell on, and they reflect the reality—the main house type on the old farms laid out by hopeful, successful southerners who came to Missouri to stay. Their construction was contemporaneous with the building of the less imposing dwellings like single-pen houses that are often considered to be the only "old pioneer homes." It is likely that the oldest house documented in Little Dixie is a magnificent half-dovetailed log central-hall I house in Howard County, which, according to family records, was built in 1816 by a Kentucky emigrant.[29] The orderly, balanced, broad central hallway and the symmetrical, vertical massing are the result of the widespread influence of the Georgian period (which had its effect in the eighteenth century in the Little Dixie source areas), and these houses are sometimes called

"Georgian subtypes." These impressive houses of the old southerners are often landmarks, the focus of family legends, Civil War stories, and (if they have been abandoned long enough to acquire the right kind of brooding atmosphere) ghost stories. In fact, two of the I houses I studied were considered haunted, one where there had been a suicide, and one where a legendary murder had occurred.

By and large, I houses were the dwellings of the Little Dixie gentry, particularly the grand central-hall subtype. Later on, the same sort of

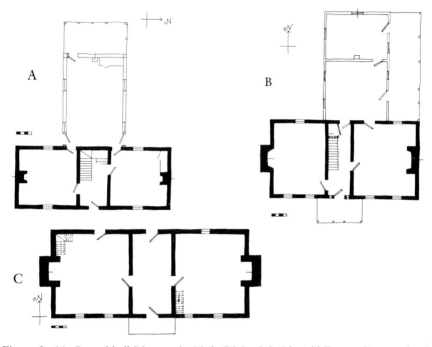

Figure 3–46. Central-hall I houses in Little Dixie. A is "the old Forrest Brown place" between Glasgow and Fayette, in Howard County, an early weatherboarded half-dove-tailed log dwelling, with front rooms smaller than average, 14' × 15' and 15' × 15', but with a usual hallway of 6'4" width. There is a full log addition to the rear that is the original kitchen, and its plastered walls are papered with old newspapers, as is the common practice. B is a V-notched log I house, weatherboarded also, on Bee Branch between Middle Grove and Madison in Monroe County. It was built by a Kentucky emigrant in about 1840 and has full brick chimneys; note that builders characteristically shifted the chimney in the gable facing the most severe winter weather to inside the gable wall to increase thermal efficiency. English emigrant Levi Keithley came from Kentucky in about 1830 and built a fine brick I house (C). Its bricks were "burned" from clay excavated on the site by slaves and laid up in common bond. It has a full limestone foundation and integral chimneys. The log ell addition (which seems to have been in the form of a saddlebag house) is now gone; the house, a rarity because it is brick and its facade is asymmetrical, is located north of Perry in Ralls County. The east room has a separate boxed-in staircase and the rear door to the missing addition, and it is possible that the slaves' quarters were in the second floor over this front room.

upwardly moving farmers, achieving success and wishing to express community stature and general well-being, built big frame pattern-book houses that followed popular or "modern" trends. Today, these farmers tend to build expensive red-brick ranch-style houses with spreading lawns of close-cropped bluegrass where the picket fences and flower borders used to be. The process of replacement began as the nineteenth century waned, and unless they were built of brick or were impressive on account of local fame or significance, these finest of Little Dixie farmhouses began to seem ordinary and old-fashioned by about 1930.

Figures 3–46 through 3–50 illustrate the range of central-hall I houses, the most significant single group of houses in Missouri. Though

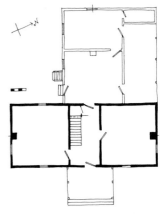

Figure 3–47. The "old Pinet house" also has a fascinating history. It is located at the site of an early French village on the Missouri River (Cote Sans Dessein) that is completely gone now, between Wainwright and Tebbetts in Callaway County. Now serving as a corncrib, the house was built in 1883 by Victor Pinet, the son of the 1830 settler Jacques Pinet, who was a foot soldier in Napoleon's army. The house has a limestone foundation and a cellar beneath the kitchen ell. The two-story portico is found on some frame I houses of the era.

they would seem much alike to a driver whizzing by on the county road, they exhibit finely tuned differences. No two are precisely the same. There is wonderful variation in what seem to be ordinary duplications of the same house. People always experiment with tradition (as they experiment with fashion), accepting, rejecting, and altering things subtly in a process that allows for personal creativity within the boundaries of tradition.

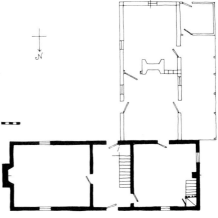

Figure 3–48. "The old Williams place" southeast of Fayette in Howard County is a half-dovetailed weatherboarded central-hall I house of early vintage for Little Dixie, 1816. Like many very early houses, there was no front porch. Its builder, Colden Williams, was a slaveholding farmer; the log kitchen addition of 1820 has a small square doorway from the kitchen to the dining room through which food was passed to the Williams family. Many slaves lived in a room of the main house, but on this farm there were several slave families, and they lived in separate log single-pen houses aligned with and facing the back porch of the kitchen addition across the sideyard and driveway.

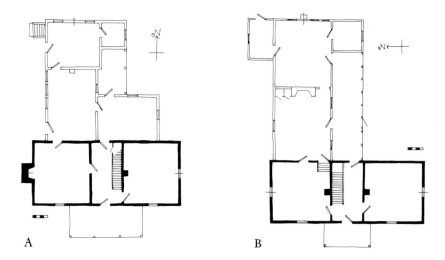

A   B

Figure 3–49. A is the Arthur Burton house, which stood between Higbee and Renick in Randolph County; the Missouri State Highway Department considered the house (used as a storage area before its demolition) to be "an eyesore" and suggested it be demolished; it was located on a small gravel road with little traffic. It was a frame central-hall I house of the "classic" Little Dixie variety, built about 1860 by a southern farmer who added several rooms to the rear, put his cold cellar beneath the far room, and located the main cooking fireplace in the east front room. The front rooms of the house (used as parlor and bedroom after the additions were made) measured 15′ × 14′6″ and 14′6″ × 14′6″, and the hall was 7′8″ wide with a broad open stairway to the second floor with finely made newel posts, banister, and balusters. Like almost every stairway in Little Dixie, this one had a storage closet underneath. B, "the old Hannah place," is a frame building west of Cairo in Randolph County with front rooms almost 15′ × 15′ separated by an 8-foot hallway. There is a full brick cooking fireplace and chimney in the kitchen ell, while small brick stove flues heat the front of the house.

Figure 3–50. A is a modest frame I house with a small 4′6″ hallway that is much like the tiny lobby entrances in similar English houses dating from the 1600s. Here the second-floor entrance is placed in a surprising but convenient place, off the back porch; the closet under the stairs opens into the little front hallway. It was built by a German Catholic emigrant, Henry Thies, on Greggs Creek between Glasgow and Steinmetz, about 1905, and is a reminder of the willingness of Germans and northerners to adopt the prevailing "southern" house types in this part of Missouri. B is a small frame house with an even smaller "hall" (2′4″), which, like the Thies house, contains a closet beneath the stairs. The house is located west of Martinsburg in Audrain County. Like many early houses, it had hinged louvered shutters outside the windows, which have fallen into disuse.

A

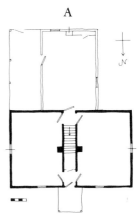

B

4
Old Barns of Little Dixie

No new house or barn types were developed in Little Dixie, but a peculiar kind of barn, known as a transverse-crib type, is widely found here and demonstrates the regional character of the region (Figure 4–1). The *transverse-crib barn* developed in the upland South as a distinct variety in the early nineteenth century and was carried across the lower Midwest by emigrating farmers and carpenters.[1] The transverse-crib barn gradually replaced other early types (like the English and the double-crib log types) in Missouri and throughout the Midwest. In form, it contains a long central driveway or passageway flanked on both sides by stables for animals and various cribs and granaries. The Creson barn in Howard County (Figure 4–2) represents the typical frame transverse-crib barn, and like almost all others of the type, this barn has been enlarged by a shed addition along one side. The roof line is parallel to the driveway, and this arrangement separates it from other barn types in the South and Midwest.

As the transverse-crib barn was built across the Little Dixie counties, a particular localization eventually developed that is distinctive for this area. This local variation on the established barn type has a forward gable extending the roof and walls outward, enclosing a space for machinery storage (where tractors are parked in bad weather) running crosswise to the barn's driveway or feedway, creating a T-shaped effect (Figure 4–3). This sort of barn, a subtype of the familiar transverse-crib form, represents a good Little Dixie creation that seems to have been mostly built by prosperous farmers, to judge from its relative size and complexity. Such variations on customary models of architectural form do occur in folk tradition, as people grapple and experiment with given materials and shapes in the process of continually refining the traditional repertoires of things, be they barns or folksongs or fiddle tunes.

Another regional variation on the firmly established transverse-crib barn type is seen in Mr. Wienhaus's barn between Mt. Airy and Clifton Hill in Randolph County (Figure 4–4). Built by a Kentucky farmer, Jim Dawson, in about 1870, this transverse-crib barn was added to by projecting the gable beyond the machinery storage area and driveway to

Figure 4–1. The Rucker brothers' frame board-and-batten transverse-crib barn south of Moberly, Randolph County, which was built about 1910 (private collection).

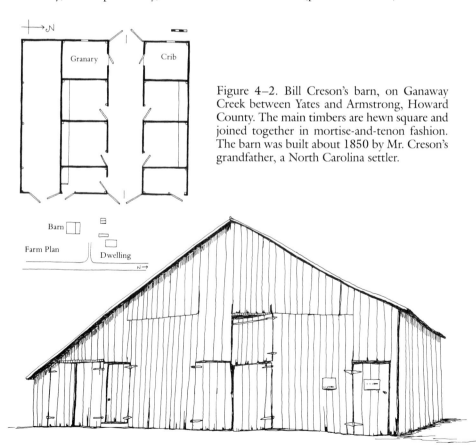

Figure 4–2. Bill Creson's barn, on Ganaway Creek between Yates and Armstrong, Howard County. The main timbers are hewn square and joined together in mortise-and-tenon fashion. The barn was built about 1850 by Mr. Creson's grandfather, a North Carolina settler.

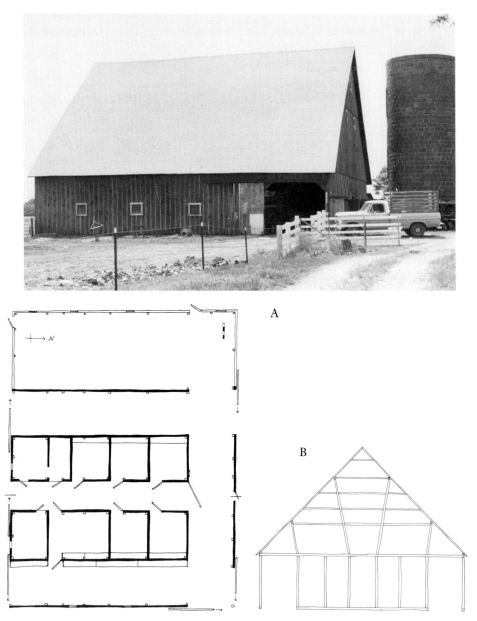

Figure 4–3. Frame transverse-crib barn on the old Marshall place on Coon Creek, Elk Fork of the Salt River between Madison and Milton, Randolph County. The main part of the building was built in about 1855 by James W. Wight (son of an 1840 emigrant from Bluegrass Kentucky); the shed along the east side was added for sheep in about 1900, and the grain silo was added in 1940. It measures 74′ × 58′ with a 7-foot driveway, an unusually large version. The main timbers are hewn square and mortised, and there are limestone footings buttressed by brick and mortar at the corners and at the stress points under the sills. The siding is the typical sort—vertical board-and-batten. B shows the bent construction in the north gable end.

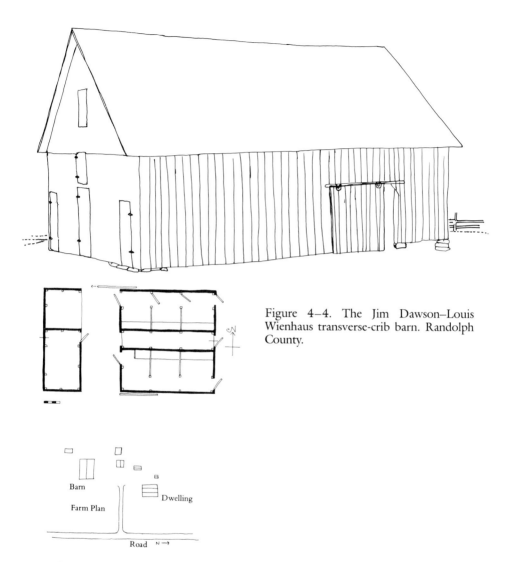

Figure 4–4. The Jim Dawson–Louis Wienhaus transverse-crib barn. Randolph County.

make space for a harness room and corncrib. Because of this functional, additive transformation, the outward appearance of the barn suggests the "English type," but the internal arrangement conforms to the transverse-crib type with its hallway or feedway running between two rows of mule stables and in line with the ridgeline of the roof. Like many nineteenth-century barns, the main vertical posts, sills, and plates are hand-hewn oak, while the lighter framing members and vertical siding are pine lumber from a sawmill. And, as in every Little Dixie barn of whatever type, there is a hayloft above the ground-floor stables, cribs, and granaries.

The kinds of transverse-crib barns range from the simple plans, like the Jim Carter barn and the Creson barn, to more complicated variations like the Tate and Marshall barns, as can be seen from the four barns shown in Figure 4–5.

Another type of barn found in the Little Dixie area, the *single-crib barn*, was also an architectural transplantation from the upland South. In this kind of barn, there is a central bay with some sort of door (dependent on its main function) flanked by small shed additions on both sides. Many of the late versions, like the Tom Hodge single-crib barn on the Earl D. Brown farm between Hallsville and Centralia in Boone County (Figure 4–6A), serve as garages and machine shops. Their most usual original functions were, however, as small hay barns, corncribs, or wagon sheds. Like other barns of different sizes and functions, single-crib barns are customarily built in vertical board-and-batten fashion. In the nineteenth century, there were a good many single-crib barns built

A

Figure 4–5. Transverse-crib barns. A is a typical frame transverse-crib barn, the standard variety, Callaway County. B is the plan of the "old Jim Carter place" between Hallsville and Murry, Boone County, which like C is wider than it is long, measuring 50′ × 24′4″ with a small 3′10″ feedway down the middle. Like others, it has a built-in granary and crib. Unlike most others, this one was not painted. C is "the old Pemberton place" operated by Mr. and Mrs. Harold B. Schofield, south of Hallsville in Boone County. Very similar to the Carter barn a few miles away, it measures 50′6″ × 23′8″ but has a larger feedway 9′10″ wide; it too is of board-and-batten unpainted construction. D is the "old Tom Hodge place" between Hallsville and Centralia, Boone County. Here there is a shed addition along one side to allow more room for sheltering livestock; built about 1880, the barn measures 60′ × 47′9″ with a 12-foot driveway large enough for wagons and tractors to pass through (delivering hay and crops); it is red with white trim.

of logs, often serving as corncribs located on the rims of cornfields far from the farmstead. The "old Schmid barn" (Figure 4–6B) is a V-notched log version on Logan Creek between Portland and Steedman, along the Missouri River bluffs in Callaway County, in the area where Little Dixie coalesces with German Missouri. Indeed, it was built by a German Lutheran immigrant farmer in about 1870.

Larger than the single-crib barns are the *double-crib barns*. These

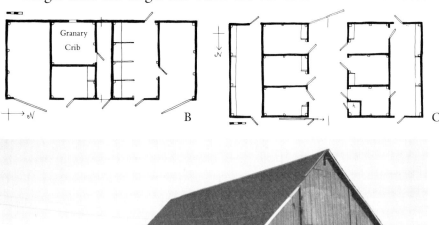

B

C

D

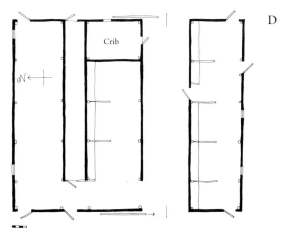

A

Figure 4–6. A, the single-crib barn on the "old Tom Hodge place" between Hallsville and Centralia in Boone County, was used as a wagon and harness shed and now serves as a garage and storage building. Most of these small frame single-crib barns serving as garages also contain the farm's machine shop and tools for repairing vehicles of all kinds. B, the "old Schmid barn," a V-notched log single-crib barn in Callaway County, built by a late German immigrant farmer. The central section is a square log unit open to the roof for the storage and protection of loose hay. In the left shed addition there are stalls and feed mangers for horses, a small, tight framed granary, and a narrow corridor. Cattle and farm machinery are sheltered in the rear section, and machinery is parked in the garage-like open shed on the right. The twin corridors, the central hay mow unit, and the granary have board floors. The log crib was not covered over on the exterior because air circulation between the logs speeds the curing and helps maintain the harvested hay.

barns always appear striking to the stranger, for, built of logs and with rambling additions, they seem out of place and decidedly old-fashioned. An early kind of barn imported into Little Dixie by southerners and Pennsylvanians as well, double-crib barns flourished in the early stages of settlement and then were almost completely replaced by their modern counterpart, the big frame transverse-crib barns of the later nineteenth and the twentieth centuries. The Binckley log double-crib barn near the Missouri River bluffs between Portland and Steedman in Callaway County is a fine example. It is built of large V-notched oak and walnut logs and has a twelve-foot driveway between the cribs (the same size as the driveways of most large transverse-crib barns). A half-dovetailed log corncrib was added later, and the roof of the main barn was continued out over the corncrib. The crib in the foreground in the photograph (Figure 4–7) is made of logs left in the round, while both the rear crib and the corncrib that was added later were built of logs that had been hewn flat on the inside and outside. There are various other frame ver-

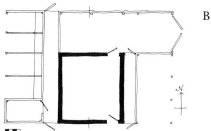

B

tical-board additions as well. A complicated barn, this double-crib barn may have started out as a single-crib barn (the portion in the foreground) and then been later enlarged by the owner. As usual, the original rived-shingle roof has been replaced by sheets of tin. In the double-crib barn, as with the other types in Little Dixie, the ground areas served as various kinds of stables, cribs, and granaries, while the hay crop was stored in the lofts above. The Ed Sapp double-crib log barn is a simpler, smaller variant of the type (Figure 4–8A). It is located between Ashland and Sapp in Boone County and was built of hewn logs joined at the corners by a standard Little Dixie method, V-notching. Its cribs measure 16′ × 16′ and 9′ × 16′, and these measurements for the barn's main cribs reflect the ancient European tradition of the sixteen-foot bay for both dwellings and barns. The driveway between the two cribs is ten feet wide, and there are frame shed additions front and rear. The "old Neff place" on Bachelor Creek between Shamrock and Bachelor in Callaway County is a V-notched double-crib barn with hewn logs that is still simpler—it lacks the shed additions on the front (Figure 4–8B). Its

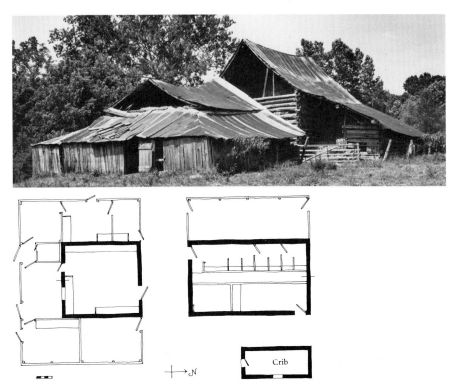

Figure 4–7. The Binckley log double-crib barn, employing fine walnut and oak logs joined by the V-notching cornering method, could be viewed as two separate single-crib barns built across an open passageway. The south log crib and its surrounding sheds resemble single-crib log barns like the Schmid barn in its arrangement and spatial functions. The two parts of this barn may have been built at slightly different times (probably by the same builders), yet the double-crib-barn form was the goal. The later addition (by different hands) was made by adding a small half-dovetailed log corncrib and extending the existing north crib's roof to shelter it too. Studies of considerable depth can be made of single structures like this that embrace intricate designs, intentions, and stages of alteration in time.

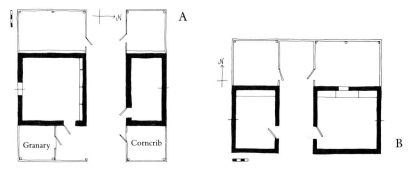

Figure 4–8. A is the Ed Sapp barn; a V-notched log double-crib barn, west of Ashland, Boone County. B is the Neff barn; a V-notched log double-crib barn, between Shamrock and Bachelor, Callaway County.

general floorplan of two main log bays divided by a driveway is the same as that found at the cores of other double-crib barns. The addition of sheds around the barn's heart does not change our identification of and satisfaction with its "type" (see also Figure 4–9). The builder of this barn came from Kentucky in about 1840.

There are also *English barns* in Little Dixie, but these are uncommon

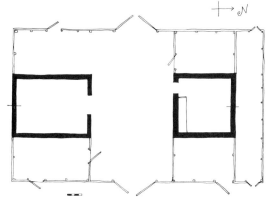

Figure 4–9. The "old Boekmann place" is a log double-crib barn south of Little Dixie's main area in the transitional zone where German influence is marked, near Argyle, Osage County. It is made of round V-notched oak logs, and its pens measure 16′ × 16′2″ and 15′5″ × 20′6″ with a wide 22′8″ driveway between. There are frame shed additions on three sides, and like Little Dixie versions, this barn has stone footings at corners and at stress points. This barn, too, from the road appears to be a frame barn, since the log cribs are hidden from view by the frame additions. It was built by the Boekmann family, German Catholic immigrants, in about 1840, and there are other log buildings on the farm, including a half-dovetailed hewn-log corncrib, a V-notched hewn-log smoke-house, a V-notched hewn-log cabin (used as a summer kitchen), and a square-notched hewn-log house.

and form only a small portion of the barn configuration. Built in frame, these small barns have two sets of stables or pens that flank a central driveway (Figure 4–10). Like Ben Cook's barn, their main timbers are usually hewn square, while the light framing members are sawed out and nailed together.

The *mountain stable* (Figure 4–11) is a barn type found in the mountainous parts of the upland South, but rarely in Missouri's Little Dixie, an area more like the Piedmont and Bluegrass than the high mountains. Generally a small frame barn, the floorplan of the mountain stable is reminiscent of the transverse-crib barn, but the ridge of the roof

Figure 4–10. English barns. A is Ben Cook's barn, in the Anabel community north of Tenmile in Macon County—outside Little Dixie's domain in its zone of transition where both northern and eastern influences are seen. It measures 37'6" × 30'6" and the drive-way is 12 feet wide. B, the Fielding barn, on Perche Creek between Harrisburg and Riggs in Boone County, is a more complicated English barn, with different shed exten-sions. C is the Wheeler barn between Moberly and Middle Grove, Randolph County, measuring 45' × 25' with a 10-foot driveway. Its main timbers were hewn square with broadaxes and were joined by mortise-and-tenon method.

runs parallel to the long sides and the main openings. In its layout it also resembles the double-crib plan. The Morton barn, in the region's western transitional zone, between Speed and Lone Elm in Cooper County, is a good example of the frame mountain stables occurring in Little Dixie. This barn measures 24′1″ × 17′9″ and has a shed added to the rear to shelter farm equipment. Too small to include cribs or granaries, it only has room for horse stalls and milk-cow stanchions.

As with their houses, farmers tend to make no complicated distinctions between "types" of barns in everyday parlance. The distinctions that are made usually fall into two kinds. The first distinction simply allows people to call barns by their main function: "horse barn," "mule barn," or "hay barn" may well apply to barns of the same design and floorplan. But the barns differ in use. Second, insiders in Little Dixie make distinctions between barns they and their neighbors have long used and the barns brought in by outsiders that seem not to fit in with the standard collection—like "Yankee barns" and "German barns." For the architecture specialist, the ways farmers classify their own structures

Crib

C

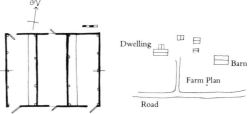

Figure 4–11. A frame "mountain stable" barn type in Cooper County; this kind of barn is common in the southern Appalachian Mountains, but not in Little Dixie or its main source areas.

are fascinating, though sometimes confusing. Thus, what may in my technical classification of barn types based on essential floorplans be called "English barns" are often known as "Yankee barns" to Little Dixie farmers, since this barn type is rather uncommon on the old southern farmsteads and seems to be found where newcomers from the east (Illinois, Ohio) or north (Iowa) settled. Moreover, the English barn type is considered to be the main traditional barn in the northeastern United States, and it is rare in the parts of the South where the Little Dixie settlers came from. Likewise, the big, complicated barns that often have "basements" and overhanging levels with ramps that specialists might call "Pennsylvania barns" are very logically called "German barns" by the farmers of Little Dixie. I saw no perfect German barns in my survey of Little Dixie, but they flourish across the Missouri River south in the areas of thick German settlement so well documented by van Ravenswaay in his study. The differences between German and "American" ("English") farmstead layouts and building types reflect the cultural backgrounds and configurations behind these carefully wrought artifacts on the land. Particular choices for the design of a barn are not due to mischief or accident. The barn is of critical importance to the success of the agricultural operation, and the right barn in the right spot is the result of a thoughtful linking of the farmer's old customs with the current patterns being built in the community. As van Ravenswaay and others have noted, the barn was the centerpiece of the farm for the German settlers, and the Germans put more effort and consideration into the location and construction of the barn than did their American neighbors.[2]

Deliberate, careful farmers, Germans customarily gave the best building site on the new farmland to the great, heavy barn, while typical Little Dixie "Americans" gave the best location to the farmhouse. The types of barns documented by van Ravenswaay as traditional and typical in German Missouri differ from the main types found north of the Missouri in Little Dixie. For the Germans, there were eight groups that van Ravenswaay shaped out of the many barns he recorded in his research: (1) log barns of one level with a driveway through the middle and hayloft above (which I term double-crib barns); (2) squarish single-crib barns on one level with lofts; (3) "Alpine or bank barns" without forebays; (4) rectangular barns of one level with doors at the gable ends and central driveways between rows of stalls (which I call transverse-crib barns); (5) Swiss-Mennonite barns with a high ramp and forebay; (6) rectangular two-level barns with lofts and doors in the gables and high ramps leading to wagon doors for the second story; (7) rectangular four-level "house-barns" built on hillsides, of German origin and exceedingly rare in the United States; and (8) "unusual designs" reflecting an idiosyncrasy or some trend.[3] I recorded examples of three of van Ravenswaay's eight types in Little Dixie: double-crib barns, single-crib barns, and transverse-crib barns (the most significant Little Dixie type). There are surely many examples of the German-type barns in Little Dixie that have yet to be located and recorded. In van Ravenswaay's study, there seem to have been too few English barns and mountain stables to warrant documentation or attention, just as the rare types in Little Dixie (one bank barn, one basement barn) went unrecorded in my own studies. Van Ravenswaay's work is important in providing comparative information for research conducted in other folk regions, and the differences between the barn types found by van Ravenswaay and the barn types that I found in Little Dixie are yet another sign of regional personality based on the cultural and ethnic ties of settlers. That kind of hard evidence found on the landscape today persuasively backs up the accounts of settlement history written in the formal record.

A

B

Figure 4–12. A, a frame slat corncrib, Boone County, red with white trim. B, a frame drive-through granary, near Hallsville, Boone County, unpainted. C, Gayle Watts enjoys the afternoon shade cast by the frame board-and-batten smokehouse and storage shed, positioned at the rear edge of the house's backyard; between Martinsburg and Benton City, Audrain County; red with white trim.

C

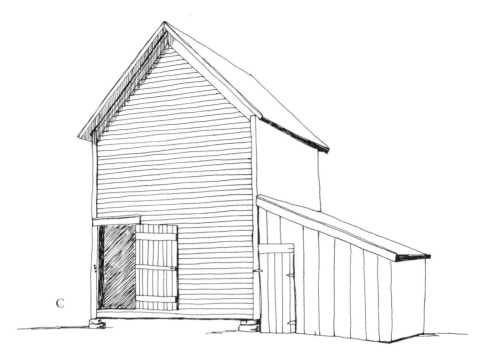

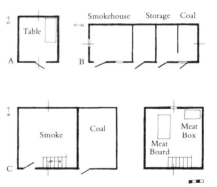

Figure 4–13. The plans of three Boone County smokehouses indicate their variety in Little Dixie. A is a frame vertical-board smokehouse between Midway and Huntsdale with a meat table for the preparation and wrapping of prepared hams and bacons. B is a frame outbuilding with horizontal lapped siding that serves several different functions, between Hallsville and Centralia. C is a two-level frame smokehouse with shed addition between Woodlandville and Hinton; meat is smoked on the ground floor, and the preparation is done on the second floor.

There are of course other kinds of agricultural outbuildings: smokehouses, granaries, corncribs, summer kitchens, cellars, washhouses (Figures 4–12 and 4–13).[4] Among the most familiar of these to Little Dixie people are the "slat" corncribs found on nearly every farm. This kind of crib, framed with light wood pieces spaced horizontally to allow air circulation around the harvested corn, is found across the South as well as in the Midwest. Figure 4–12A shows a slat crib between Hallsville and Centralia in Boone County. Though granaries for crops of soybeans, wheat, rye, milo, and other grains are often contained inside large barns like the transverse-crib type, there are many that stand alone, like this drive-through granary south of Hallsville in Boone County (Figure 4–12B). In drive-through granaries, the loaded wagons can be pulled directly between the sets of grain bins for easy off-loading of the harvest. Figure 4–12C shows a frame smokehouse in the Watts's farmyard located between Martinsburg and Benton City in Audrain County.

The barns and other agricultural buildings that form much of the visible architectural pattern on the rural landscape capture the attention of the traveler, the writer, and the photographer. They often seem a haphazard batch of merely functional and pleasing structures. Yet in different areas of the nation particular assemblages of farm buildings exhibit, as in Little Dixie, the imprint of the cultural traditions in each place that give them what we think of as regional personality.

5
A Note on Construction
Methods and Materials

The land, a particular environment with particular resources, is given. Cultural landscapes are made as people carve into the forests and prairies, making culture from nature. The enormous forests that met European builders everywhere, from Colonial times to the present, became the actual basis for civilization, and all sorts of woodworking skills became "a fine art."[1] By the time the Little Dixie region was settled in the early nineteenth century, the general level of wood-handling skills was very high and such skills were very widespread. Not only did the architectural equipment of the new Missourians include mental blueprints for certain traditional buildings they wished to replicate in their new land, but almost every pioneering family had a member with passable knowledge of carpentry. But, remember that the familiar stereotype of the noble pioneer with his trusty ax hacking down the mighty oaks and throwing together lovely cabins in the woods is preposterous and wrong. There were always specialists with special woodworking tools and experience to do the finish work necessary to have a fine house or log cabin. The number of hand tools required to build the average permanent log house is at least fifty and may run to nearly eighty. That trusty ax and noble courage would get one a temporary shelter of rough chopped trees piled together and little else.[2] Further, all of the traditional methods of construction in Missouri have European antecedents: weatherboarding over heavy frame or a balloon frame, horizontal log construction, brick, stone, half-timbering, and vertical log construction (absent in Little Dixie but present in the old French settlements of the state).[3] Though "invented" in Chicago around 1835, the so-called balloon frame of light, sawed timbers forming a skeletal box also has European sources. But the Midwest is a land of wood, and an architecture of wooden construction dominates almost everywhere, even in midwestern subregions where there were considerable influxes of settlers with brick or stone traditions. Of the several modes of construction available to newcomers in Missouri, two ways of dealing with wood came to completely dominate the scene—building in weatherboarded frame, and building in horizontal logs (left round or hewn). Building in brick is uncommon in the countryside and is pretty much limited to impressive I houses, most of which were the seats of successful farmers who were slaveholders. No brick buildings were recorded during my field research that did not predate the Civil War, and the two brick houses I documented were said to have been built by slave labor with bricks "burned" from earth dug up for the dwellings' foundations. My examination of the bricks (particularly their uneven texture, density, and color) and the building sites confirmed this belief, commonly expressed by people in the region. As in ancient British tradition, there seems to be a significant, deep-seated inner preference for wooden buildings, even in places like Little Dixie—or Wales—where stone of very high quality is available.[4]

There seem to be no stone houses or barns in abundance in Little Dixie. Though I recorded none in my work, there could well be examples in existence. Stone buildings occur just over the river in the richly German settlement areas. In the buildings I studied, the use of limestone was restricted to cornerstones or piers supporting sills, to chimneys (Figure 5–1), fireplace hearths and boxes, doorsteps, and foundations for two-level outbuildings erected on sloping ground. Good limestone is easily available in many corners of the Little Dixie region, but the settlers had no strong stonemasonry tradition when they first came to Little Dixie. Even today, the limestone being blasted out of quarries in the region is generally ground up and used as gravel, not as construction stone.

Whether by German or by American hands, few examples of half-timbering stand today. Three half-timbered houses with hand-hewn box framing were recorded for this book: a saddlebag house overlooking the Missouri River in Boone County, a slightly rectangular stack-house type in Monroe County, and a central-hall house in Montgomery County (Figure 5–2). In these buildings, the brick nogging or infill serves more as insulation against the weather than as a structural feature as it might in "true" half-timbering in England or the *Fachwerk* buildings both in Germany and in van Ravenswaay's German Missouri. Other kinds of infill (stones or wattle and daub) were not discovered in Little Dixie. There are antecedents for half-timbering with hand-hewn structural members and nogging for insulation in Germany and England as well as in earlier times in the American colonies. This imported mode of construction was used in the Peyton Randolph house in Williamsburg, Virginia, and the look of it resembles Little Dixie half-timbering.[5] In Andrew Jackson Downing's attempt to foist fashion on farmers, *The*

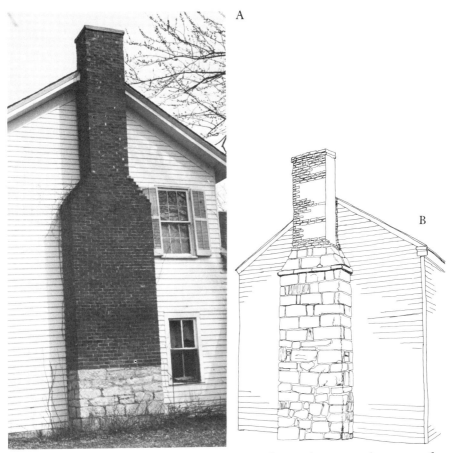

Figure 5–1. A shows how limestone blocks were often used as supporting courses for "English" brick chimneys; this one is between Huntsdale and Rocheport in Howard County. B shows the most impressive chimney I recorded, on the Kleasner log I house between Boonesboro and Fayette, Howard County.

Architecture of Country Houses, there is advice to fill the vertical spaces between wall studding with brick nogging: "To make the cottage comfortable for the north, it should be filled-in with soft bricks, placed on edge, so as to allow the inside wall to be plastered on the brick."[6] For Missouri, we do not know yet whether German immigrants are responsible for Little Dixie half-timbering or whether the method was used by the Anglo-Americans from the first. Most architectural historians would be surprised to find half-timbering off in the hinterland of Little Dixie and would say it was the work of immigrant German craftsmen, but I would tend to disagree based on the bits of evidence recorded.

The period of "box framing," employing a system of great hewn

Figure 5–2. Interior and exterior views of half-timbering with brick nogging between outer weatherboarding and inner plastering, in a central-hall house near Gamma, Montgomery County; sills and corner posts were hewn logs made square.

timbers mortised together, was brief in Little Dixie. The deep change from box-framing to balloon-framing techniques had occurred by the time of heavy Missouri settlement before the Civil War. By the 1870s, balloon-frame construction had become the United States's main folk-construction mode.[7] The spread of the balloon-frame technique required the presence of local sawmills and cheap wire nails, both of which were available in Little Dixie soon after settlement began. The abundance of outstanding hardwood for the sawyer's business made the spread of both balloon-frame construction and log construction more significant in this region.

When houses are made of logs in Little Dixie, the horizontal timbers are always hewn flat on two sides and then joined at the corners by one of three methods: V-notching (most widespread), half-dovetailing (next in occurrence), or square-notching (rare here). The fourth important Little Dixie log corner-timbering method, saddle-notching, is used only for logs left round, which are found in barns and other agricultural structures. The manner of log hewing in Little Dixie is the same as that in the upland South, basically a two-fold sequence of scoring with a felling ax followed by "hewing to the line" with a broadax. Chinking of the interstices between the logs is with mud or clay and stones, sticks, or shingles, and usually the chinking is plastered smoothly over on the interior walls with a lime-based plastering material concocted by the builder—"hog-hair plaster" and "horse-hair plaster," for example. Most log houses were covered on the outside with horizontal lapped weatherboards soon after construction was completed, though several were not. Large log houses are always sided; it is the small cabins that are sometimes left unprotected. Log houses, especially early ones, have outside end chimneys centered in the gable (built in limestone or some combination of stone at the bottom and brick at the top or built completely in brick). Later examples have brick stove chimneys, generally eighteen inches square and centered in the gable inside the wall. Flooring is of wide boards or planks nailed over the floor joists. Fancy floors are made of narrow tongue-and-groove boards. Flooring is nailed down over the joists, which often are logs hewn flat only on the top side or on the top and bottom sides. The inside walls are either bare, whitewashed logs, or papered, or covered with vertical boards or wainscoting. The most usual wood used in log construction here is white oak, but black walnut was also used and even preferred when easily available in the old stands of first-growth walnut in the hardwood forests across the region. Fine log I houses of walnut can be seen, and central Missouri walnut timber is highly prized today for the making of gun stocks and furniture. Other kinds of wood were not used as often as oak and walnut. Tulip poplar was used elsewhere (for example, in southern Indiana), but this tree is rare in Little Dixie. Weatherboarding is often of walnut on early houses and pine on later ones. Interior lathing for plastering is frequently of rived oak. If the house is frame, its main vertical timbers are sometimes hewn and joined. Frame houses, like most log houses, are covered with horizontal lapped siding. In log houses, the logs stop at the roofline. All of the log houses studied in Little Dixie had gable roofs with the house's front door in the long side and parallel to the ridge of the roof. The plates in these buildings (the top horizontal timber in the front and rear wall, supporting the roof system) are often hewn square and set out over the walls to provide additional protection for the building. The two gables of the houses are constructed of frame (with vertical studs) and covered with either vertical or horizontal weatherboarding or wide boards. Lofts are usually unheated and used for storage or sleeping quarters for youngsters in the family. Entrance to the loft is usually via a boxed-in stairway with a small low closet underneath, sometimes referred to as "the under the stairs" (Figure 5–3), and rarely by ladder through an opening in the ceiling. Pitch roofs were built using rafter couples butted at the peak and joined by an open mortise-and-tenon joint. Rafters often are skinned or unskinned six-inch poles. Collar beams increase the rigidity of the common rafter system. Wide decking boards are nailed horizontally over the rafters and then hand-rived shingles are nailed in courses over the decking to produce a tight roof. The belief is that such an old-fashioned shingle roof will last fifty years if put on right. Most houses have a kitchen shed addition to the rear. Some have lateral additions, creating other house types.

The surprisingly large number of fine log buildings in Little Dixie helps show its kinship with the areas from which most of its settlers traveled, the Bluegrass and the Piedmont, regions where log construction predominated as in no other American localities.[8] Although log construction is found all over the state of Missouri, its intensity and high quality in the Little Dixie section are striking. In my field research I studied some fifty log buildings, representing almost half of the total number of structures documented. There are hundreds of log houses and barns still in use today, though the logs are likely to be camouflaged beneath sawed weatherboards that protect them from the elements of nature and the elements of man. The log-construction imprint is strongest in the first areas settled, and the greatest quantity surviving the years of decay, disuse, and fradulent historic preservation are located in isolated ranks of rolling hills and hollows, mostly along the Missouri River.

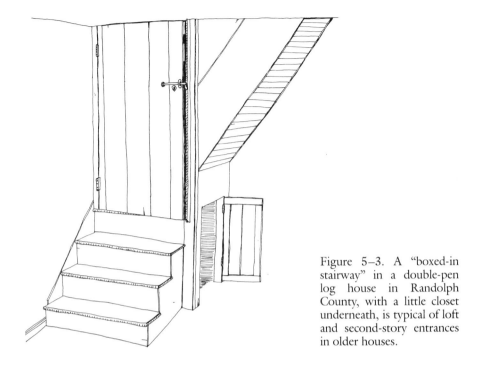

Figure 5–3. A "boxed-in stairway" in a double-pen log house in Randolph County, with a little closet underneath, is typical of loft and second-story entrances in older houses.

In terms of house types and log construction, almost all the log single-pen houses are V-notched, but stack houses, double-pen houses, central-hall houses, and I houses are as likely to be half-dovetailed or, less often, square-notched. Dogtrot houses were either square-notched or half-dovetailed. A full investigation that would comprise a study in itself could be done to determine the correlation between cornering methods and house types and between cornering methods and the application of weatherboarding. I suggest that V-notching (considered by some to be the simplest of the main four cornering methods) tended to be used in smaller and less substantial house types, like single-pen houses, and that the more intricate half-dovetailing and square-notching techniques were used in more sizable and carefully designed—and sometimes earlier—houses. Close examination of the actual buildings shows great care, though, even in the most modest single-pen houses, and the evidence from my field research significantly proves two important points about building in log: first, log houses and barns are *not* simple to build, and second, they were built soundly and made to last many generations (Figure 5–4).[9]

The fluorescence of log building in Little Dixie seems to have been from about 1825 to 1860, after which the spread of local sawmills

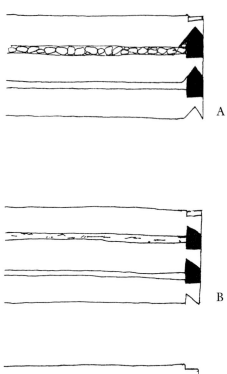

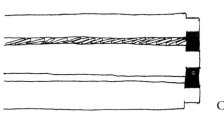

Figure 5–4. Log corner-timbering techniques in Little Dixie houses. A. V-notching (with stones for chinking, for demonstration purposes). B. Half-dovetailing (with mud chinking). C. Square-notching (with stick chinking). Chinking material revealed in the drawing is plastered over in actuality.

(water and steam driven) and cheap manufactured nails made frame construction more available to builders and farmers. It is notable that in Little Dixie a good log house (properly sided), particularly if a large one, was intended to be *the* house, not a temporary dwelling. Settlers with limited means built smaller but still carefully hewn log cabins, and these were almost always enlarged by frame additions as soon as the farmer was able to make alterations to his first house. The small single-pen houses were the result of temporary poverty, but they were not temporary housing. Periodic additions of rooms to a basic one-room plan often created rambling, large houses with plenty of space for all purposes. Popular stereotypes and images of the nineteenth century, carried on in media representations today, have helped create a false image of crude, rough log shacks that right-thinking pioneers soon put behind them. Satires and parodies of the settlement period often give humorous depictions, but in contemporary America we lack the knowledge and perception of the mood and reality of those times, so innocent readers of "history" and archival collections miss the original pointed humor. In "Texan Boys," a fine Missouri folk ballad from James Ashby's Holt County songbook of 1906, the rowdies from Texas inhabit what people today would assume to be a typical log house, but which was not at all typical:

> The house they live in is hewed out logs,
> Hewed out logs and a puncheon floor,
> A clapboard roof and a rawhide door.[10]

There were, of course, rough temporary log cabins like the ones in the popular image, houses laid up quickly with only a few tools. Round logs were used, and the cabins were saddle-notched, unsided, and did contain puncheon floors and rough board roofs. So far as I can determine, none of these has survived into the present century. And in Little Dixie, a region in which exceptionally high log-construction standards were embedded in the community's architectural traditions, there were probably never very many of those scrappy cabins we see in contemporary pioneer movies and television programs. The most modest log dwellings still in use in Little Dixie are made of carefully hewn oak or walnut logs and finished with details fine enough to impress the most famous modern cabinetmaker.

Mr. Jake Griffin, of Ashland, Boone County, gave me a good account of how he and some neighbors built his first farmhouse, a rectangular log single-pen house (Figure 5–5), in 1908:

> Well, we built this ole house down in Fox Holler, this ole log house. Built it myself. Built that house on a dollar and a half. Dollar and a half of money. Come here t' Ashland with a dollar and a half's worth of nails t' build a house.
>
> *Mrs. Griffin:* Hewed it himself. Made the boards, too, t' cover the roof.
>
> *Jake Griffin:* Yup. Chinked it up, and put lime in *that*. Lay that chinkin' wood on top of each other. Split that out and cover with lime.
>
> *Marshall:* How'd you make your lime?
>
> *Jake Griffin:* Made a log heap, and put the rock in there, and burn 'em. When I got it burnt, I took it down to where I built the house, and dug me a hole in the ground and run that lime off in the ground, then run

water on it and let it slack up there. Then I just covered it up, and left it a long time, till I got ready to use it. Then ya mix it with sand, and that's it. . . . Used to be an ole man over here name of George Zumwalt, and he *burnt* lime—had a big hole in the ground like a well, and he'd go haul this lime rock and wall that up in there, all solid, and leave just a place big enough to burn cordwood. Burn them rocks, and man, he'd have a lot of lime when he got done. That was his business, burnin' lime—it'd take him about two weeks or more t' burn it. Then he'd sell it or trade it to ya.

Marshall: . . . how'd you learn to make those corners, and build your house, and all?

Jake Griffin: Well, I just took it up. Had an uncle, a tiemaker—he hewed ties [railroad crossties]—so I'd seen him hew ties, and I'd seen logs that'd been hewed. Had a house raisin'. One man on each corner, and they'd notch th house down. Notch the logs as each log goes up on. That top log, you gotta cut it just so, and then you gotta cut the next log just to fit right over it—like a V. They'd use an ax to cut the corners. Use a *broad* ax for hewin' the logs flat, though. Used oak, mostly, red oak. Then ya have skid poles, and ya get way up high with the logs, and just shove 'em up to it. Take a stick and just push 'em up. It took about five fellers just to *seat* 'em—them was right smart of weight. Well, you'd just have a *house-raisin'* an' all the neighbors would come. They'd be fifteen or twenty men. Yeh, an' the women would cook, and have a big party afterwards. I've had a wood-choppin', and I'd have a dance that night.

Marshall: What's a wood-choppin'?

Jake Griffin: Well, it's just to cut *cordwood*—or any kinda wood ya want. I've cleaned up ground. Before I built that house down there, I bought land, bought seventy acres, and 'twas all in timber. And I'd have workins and give the boys a *dance* that night. Had fiddlin' and guitars. . . . I used to play the french harp pretty good.[11]

Attitudes toward old log buildings are mixed. "City people" (those living in towns of any size) tend to admire them. Farmers are usually uninterested. A number of log cabins and small log houses were converted from dwellings to equipment sheds, summer kitchens, or corncribs years ago, and many good log houses have been dismantled or burned down in the past several years. As a product of the back-to-the-land movement inspired by *The Whole Earth Catalog* and the current search for dwellings with inherent energy-efficient design and fabrication factors, log-cabin building is undergoing a phase of popularity like it did in the 1930s, when conditions of Depression times made log construction temporarily logical again and when the U.S. Forest Service built scores of "rustic" (their term) log cabins, mostly in the West and almost

Figure 5–5. Mr. Griffin's house, a V-notched log single-pen type in Fox Hollow near Ashland, Boone County; 1908.

always of round, saddle-notched logs suitable and appropriate for alpine western forest offices and camps but in a tradition very different from those of the East and especially the Midwest. Most of the current interest has led to pale, outrageous, and embarrassing imitations of authentic log construction, and the trend is fired by a flow of misguided and sometimes deceptive books and articles.[12] Like Mr. Griffin's oral testimony based on personal experience, there are accounts that can be studied (and generally appreciated) for their accurate and realistic descriptions of log building.[13] It is essential to an improved comprehension of historic truth that log cabins and construction be understood not as some jolly survival of some imaginary primitive pioneer era but—as the elegant evidence of field research proves—as a complicated and systematic order of building that offers significant meanings to scholars and students of cultural expression. What seems casually to be a simple log hut may be read as a complex and evocative document containing interesting messages about how people conceived of shelter, of craftsmanship, of self-image, of life.

On Paint and Other Matters

Every frame farmhouse recorded in Little Dixie was either painted white (or whitewashed) or through aging had turned from white to gray. Brick farmhouses are naturally red or painted dark blue or white. They originally were unpainted. Barns, regardless of type and if painted, are red or white. Houses very rarely are not painted; barns often are not. Outbuildings also are often unpainted, except when they are positioned close to the farmhouse and are a part of the formal "farmyard" (summer kitchens, smokehouses, cellar houses, washhouses). But in the same farmyard the cellar house may be painted white and the smokehouse left unpainted. Exterior house trim (window sashes, doorjambs, shutters, cornices, porch railings) is often brightly or contrastingly painted, and so is interior trim. Picket fences fronting farmhouses are painted white or whitewashed; "board fences" separating farmyard from barnyard may or may not be painted, but if painted are also white. In addition, the various secondary parts of the farmyard constellation of artifacts may be wildly colored: mailboxes, wind toys, garden and path rock borders, rear axle tractor tires used as flower boxes, and the like.[14]

Architectural specialists who do field research today and cope with American folk buildings worry less about precise dating than about documenting and analyzing cultural process, change, regional patterning, and aspects of the community. Indeed, for a great many folk buildings, there is little possibility of establishing the kinds of dating and formal history that we develop when we research academic architecture. A great fuss is occasionally made over particular buildings—Abraham Lincoln's boyhood home in Illinois or Harry Truman's birthplace in Lamar, Missouri—but for those buildings fixing the probable decade of construction would be sufficient. Traditional architecture is patterned geographically and culturally, not chronologically.[15]

The impressions conveyed by public buildings differ from those conveyed by houses, and the symbolic divergence between public and private is enacted in rural public buildings (Figures 5–6 and 5–7). The way houses are presented is very different from the way public buildings, like churches and barns, are presented. The separation between houses where people live and buildings where people work or conduct community affairs is a cleavage of private architectural form and space from public form and space. This different way of thinking is reflected in the way traditional churches and the places for commerce and discourse tend to be turned so that the triangular, vertical gable faces the road or street. All of the folk *houses* in Little Dixie come out of the very old European custom of presenting the long side of the dwelling to the public eye. The difference between the private, inside world of a home and the public, outside world of a rural church or Masonic lodge is clear from the gable-out facades of these public structures, which seem to be taller, more ambitious, and more impressive—just like the Greek temples whose hallowed frontal design is retained in the simplified and clarified reduction of the ancient architectural style revived and made significant in the nineteenth century in the midwestern United States.

How old is "old" in central Missouri? A house built in 1820 is old in central Missouri, and it is significant that many people believe much newer houses to be equally ancient. Particularly with folk houses, conforming as they do to established traditional "types" known and built over many generations to much the same plans, many houses indeed appear to date from the early nineteenth century that were built after 1900. Antique dealers usually say that an object needs to be fifty years old to make the antique grade. Old-car collectors say that twenty years of age is sufficient to warrant "antique" status. My six-year-old son thinks our 1970 television set is a rickety old relic. Indeed, all are correct, for the way people judge age is a complicated and psychological matter disobeying all rules. A house considered very old in northern California is thought to be ridiculously new when judged by the conceits of Tidewater Virginia and Maryland historians. It is the community belief system that counts the most in sorting out dates for Little Dixie buildings, and long-held opinion is equivalent in value to the outsider's meticulous searches through records. Certainly historic "dates" are truly important, but our search is in regional folklife and not formal history. In my research, I naturally tended to become interested in buildings that were clearly in the "old" category, since folk architecture in this part of the Midwest underwent important changes and deletions of traditional types around the time of the First World War, and this work ultimately

A

Figure 5–6. A is the Antioch Church, near Milton, Randolph County, with its new steeple in place. The church was organized in 1837, and the structure is the frame 1897 one built to replace the log church that burned. B shows the interior during Sunday communion, July 1979.

B

Figure 5–7. Community meetings and suppers by groups such as the Masons and their families take place in the Milton Lodge in Randolph County, established in 1855. Current members like Thomas J. Marshall (a descendant of early members, pictured with nephew Sandy in 1978) take pride in maintaining the venerable structure, which is a local landmark. The building was originally a store, dating to about 1840, and has been in continual use in this once-lively rural town on the first trail and road west from Hannibal to Glasgow on the Missouri River.

grapples with the nineteenth century and its spillover into memory in the twentieth.

Van Ravenswaay's work in the German settlement region on Little Dixie's southern and southeastern perimeter is extremely valuable as a companion study to this one, as actual field research in both "regions" provides materials for future studies as well as delimiting two adjacent and yet fuzzy folk-regional landscapes. There are certain resonances between Little Dixie and German Missouri—in the preponderance of the V-notching technique in log construction and in the revelation that in both places the German builders accepted and adopted the flourishing Anglo-American modes of log building. And here, too, is a glowing case of the perfect "American" combination, the syncretism of differing cultural traditions: German woodworking skills and British house forms. German woodworking techniques and British house types met and coalesced in the Pennsylvania and valley of Virginia settlement areas on the Colonial frontier. Just as Pennsylvania Germans settled alongside Scotch-Irish settlers in earlier times, a similar meeting took place on the nineteenth-century Missouri frontier. But here, the British-American pioneers had already acquired the old Germanic woodworking techniques, and what took place was an interesting switch in which the southerners of British stock demonstrated log construction for the new group of Germans, many of whom by midcentury lacked the traditional knowledge. So the southerners and British-American pioneers retaught German woodworking to the new German settlers.[16]

It is through the pain and excitement of field research today that we finally will cause new histories to be written that will bring traditional life and work into sharp and telling focus. Far from being another hilly expanse of the general Midwest, this region that many people still call Little Dixie may come into its own. It surely represents a clear, tangible extension of traditional architectural patterns intentionally transplanted from Virginia, North Carolina, and Kentucky by the first waves of farmers who came to stay. Here, the old brick central-hall I houses are "old southern mansions" both for insiders and outsiders alike.

6
Architecture and the Sense of Place

Mr. Clarence L. Klink, Huntsville, Randolph County, aged eighty-five in 1974:

> This right here is Little Dixie. Call it that because of all the Kentucky and Virginia folks settled in here way before the war. The old timers always said how much they liked it when they seen it. Just like back home. And they even made their houses just the same as back where they come from.

Mr. A. L. Steinmiller, Paris, Monroe County, aged seventy-two in 1971:

> Never heard of it. Them Americans call me *krauthead!* Democrats? They're as crooked as a bed o' *snakes!*

Mrs. Gertrude Cottingham, Renick, Randolph County, aged sixty-eight in 1974:

> Don't know for sure why they call it that—probably because it's always gone Democrat, like the *rest* of the South. I guess it's Randolph, Monroe, and maybe Howard County—and maybe Chariton, Macon, Boone, Audrain, too. Everybody just takes it for granted that we're Little Dixie. I first heard the term used in 1928, I remember that.

Mrs. Vineta Dutton, Fulton, Callaway County, aged sixty in 1974:

> Little Dixie? Now, I should know. I'm a schoolteacher. But I don't.

Little Dixie is the world with your county in the middle. Like every American cultural region, its particular history and personality affect the people who live there. When I began the field research for this study and started asking questions about the identity and character of this place, it soon became clear that beyond the importance of the old architectural patterns of "southern" building types and techniques, there was a broad knowledge among people I visited with that this was a genuine insider's region, different from the areas around it. Moreover, I discovered that while many people have finely honed attitudes and special definitions of Little Dixie, many who are longtime residents know nothing and care nothing about the sort of "history" that intrigues some of us so much.

Figure 6–1. Mr. and Mrs. Gayle Watts on their farm in Audrain County.

There is little agreement over the precise boundaries or the specific counties that should be included in the region, and it is significant that about half of those I talked with thought Little Dixie was really their home county only. The minimum definition, then, calls for the one county in which you live, and wider definitions ramble all the way "from here to old Mexico!"[1] Of the hundred formal answers to my pointed questions, sixteen people had heard of Little Dixie but had no knowledge of its borders, and eleven who had lived on the same farm all their lives had never heard the term used. I find it fascinating that people tend not to think much about exact limits for the region in which they live and work. People certainly have keen perceptions of how their ways of doing things differ from the ways of the Germans or of the Yankee farmers up in Iowa, but most people do not carve out definitions of their geographical areas. If you ask a person about Little Dixie, his first and most natural response is to name his county of residence, for there the insider's concepts of private and community personality often begin. The next round of reflection leads people to add the names of the counties adjoining their home county. Some responses show how people have pondered the Little Dixie scene for many years, and these people—usually descendants of pioneer families—have intricate, fascinating definitions based on the experiences of their family or on other personal knowledge gained through oral tradition in their community contexts.

In the counties outside the eight Little Dixie counties, about half of the people interviewed knew about the region and the term, with definitions ranging from "up around Moberly and Fulton" for a Cole County farmer living south across the Missouri River to "south of here" for a farmer living in Macon County on Little Dixie's northern transition zone.[2]

The origin of the Little Dixie name was consistently attributed to two things: the southern background and historic orientation of the region, and its famous political ties with the Democratic party. Most people say that southern traditions are the principal factor in the area's regional character, and many cite both rationales. The majority of the people living in this section of central Missouri believe they are a part—actively and willingly or passively—of the Little Dixie tableau. Some stoutly deny it. Mere residence in the region certainly does not automatically mean participation in the traditional belief system that operates around the notion of a "little Dixie." On the contrary, there are those whose families have been farming that ground for 150 years and have no particular interest in it. But every person I talked with in about 125 interviews over several years' time was knowledgeable about the southern background and basic outlines of settlement history even if he had never heard the term *Little Dixie* used.

The mention of the term to some people quickly activates memories about the old days, which many still consider a kind of "golden age." And knowledge and participation in oral traditions about Little Dixie are not completely governed by ethnic or cultural ties. It is a matter of opportunity, and a matter of choice. You can learn about Little Dixie through the customary pipelines of oral circulation or you may hear the term used over the radio or see it printed in newspaper stories and advertisements often enough to remember it. In addition to being continually used in regional newspapers published in Mexico (Audrain County), Moberly (Randolph County), Columbia (Boone County), and Paris (Monroe County), the term *Little Dixie* crops up often in radio programs broadcast by locally operated stations like KXEO in Mexico, KWIX in Moberly, and KFAL in Fulton.

More samples from conversations with a range of people hint at the variety and provocative complexity of attitudes toward Little Dixie.

> Little Dixie? Oh, my goodness yes. It's all Democrats here. Monroe County is the banner Democratic county in the whole state. It's Randolph,

Monroe, Shelby, Audrain, Ralls, and Marion—where all the slave-holding people lived. This county is the *center* of it.

This is Little Dixie country. Never knew for sure where it started and where it stopped. Grandpaw on mother's side fought in the Union army, and the other grandfather fought on the Southern side. Little Dixie is Monroe, Audrain. Because of the Southern sympathy. Ten times as many men went to the Southern army than to the North. . . . That old log house we looked at down there was the Confederate headquarters during the Civil War—they had skirmishes back and forth. It's on "horseshoe bend" and there was an old water mill there, too. *We never forgot the war* in *this* country.

Don't know why. Folks came here from Illinois in 1906—they were mixed pickles.

Little Dixie is Monroe, Ralls, Pike, Shelby, Audrain, Randolph, Howard, Boone, Chariton, and maybe Callaway and Marion. Called that because of the Kentucky and Virginia background. North of here there are Germans, and Scandinavians—also further south, there are Pennsylvania Dutch, across the river. The Democratic party is very strong here, too. Some of the old-timers were slave keepers and some weren't. My grandfather had 'em—but my other grandfather in Ralls County didn't. *The Mexico Ledger* claims that it's the capital of Little Dixie, but it's *here*. During the war there were many more Confederate sympathizers here than Northern.

Paris has *always* been known as Little Dixie. All of Monroe County. Never heard too much mention of it. My great-grandfather came here to Missouri from Ireland in 1838, through Kentucky, Patrick Whelan.

Sure, like she said. My grandfather fit in the war, and the Yankees throwed him in *prison*.

Little Dixie's Randolph, Howard, Monroe, Audrain, and Boone. Heard it as a boy. Call it that because of all the southern folks in here, and because of politics. My great-grandfather came to Howard County from Virginia— went through Kentucky—before the war. Had fifteen slaves.

Little Dixie's Randolph County. . . . because of the Mason-Dixon Line, ran right through here, and the war.

Dang right this is Little Dixie! Randolph County! Been called that 'cause of the Southerners, and the Democrats in here.

Well, I'm the last Wight in the County, here, and these stories were passed on to me by my grandfather, telling about *his* father, which would be my great-grandfather and your great-great-grandfather. Stories that took place before and after the Civil War. . . . There was a Southern soldier that was trying to get back to the Southern lines. And my great-grandfather had given him a horse, and they had it saddled and tied up there. And they was gonna put him up for the night, upstairs there. And they were fixing to go to bed. And at that time down at old Milton, that old town there, most of the time there were Union soldiers there. The regular Southern soldiers were further south. And I can't remember his name—he wanted to get back to the Southern lines. And Paw-Paw—now, we children called him Paw-Paw, and other folks knew him as Captain Wight—aimed to help him. And they were just getting ready to go to bed, and they heard a bunch of soldiers ride up into the yard. And they were kind of afraid something like that'd happen. Like I say, they had a horse tied up out there on the fence, saddled and everything, in case he wanted to get away in a hurry. And the soldier said, "Throw the door wide open and you git back out of the way. I'm not gonna let them capture me, I'm coming outa here!" And he come down those big stairs—that stairway was right close to the side door out onto the porch. And he came down those stairs. Said he throwed the door wide open, and a gun in each hand, and ran out a-shootin'. And those soldiers out there kinda scattered and he ran and jumped on this horse and took off and they were after him. But he got away on this horse and got back to the Southern line. Now that's the way the story was told to me. And that story really fascinated me, after going out and living there, and there was that same old stairway. . . . Little Dixie's Monroe County, and Randolph County, and Howard County, and Boone County. 'Cause they was mostly from Kentucky, and Virginia—southerners. And I don't suppose Randolph County has ever voted anything but Democratic. . . . And 'course, Columbia, it's changed a lot—in fact, they've elected some Republicans there the last few years—there have never been any officials other than Democratic in Boone County until just recently. Chariton County kinda belongs in there, too. And, yes, Audrain, sort of. And of course as far as *southern* counties, *Howard* County, and Monroe.

Little Dixie's Boone, Callaway, Audrain, 'cause it's always been Democrat, up till the last election right here. This *used* to be the Kingdom of Callaway here—during the Civil War this county went for the *South* and set up a kingdom of their *own*. Named for ole Captain Callaway, who come from Kentucky or Tennessee. Sure is heavy Democratic vote here. Sixty years ago there was only forty-one Republicans in the whole county.

Sure, this is Little Dixie. Heard it way back. My grandfather entered that land [farm near Shamrock] at Palmyra. Come here from Kentucky in 1832, settled first down near Lexington. Didn't have any slaves. He come with his brother Will, on horseback. My dad fit in the War—he enlisted on his twenty-first birthday, at the big elm tree in front of Board's big house. Henry Burt was captain. Then he made his way in to Price's army, and he was put in Joe Shelby's cavalry. Shelby made the boast that he could outrun anything he couldn't *whip*! Tough ole *Confederates*! Ole Colonel Jefferson Jones trained the local boys in the War—and he was interested in Little

Dixie years after the War. That Yankee militia—just a bunch of durn thieves is what they were. . . . It's here, and over in Monroe County, and Audrain—and heck, all over that country.[3]

For farmers and townspeople alike, Little Dixie is a name that can convey a meaningful sense of place, a sense of belonging, of inheritance, and a connection (dimly or sharply perceived) based on a selective community memory of a common past kept alive for current and future uses. No one knows when the term was first used, but it was probably widespread in the 1880s. Little Dixie has no commonly repeated or standard "place-name story," but the belief and the attitude are more important than some set repertoire of narratives. The name operates as a label for regional awareness based both on actual history and on impressionistic history, and as a device for public and commercial interests. There is a Little Dixie square-dance club, a Little Dixie Inn, a Little Dixie womens' study group, and a Little Dixie Library system. There are Little Dixie Shriners, a Little Dixie Art Association, Little Dixie Eggs, Little Dixie Fried Chicken, a Little Dixie Citizens' Band Radio Club, a Little Dixie Bluegrass Festival, a state-owned Little Dixie Lake, and there is Little

Figure 6–2. Mr. Christy Burks holding a wasps' nest, on his farm on Terrapin Creek, between Rocheport and Huntsdale, Boone County.

Figure 6–3. Musicians at Little Dixie Bluegrass Festival, Centralia, 1974.

Dixie Ham. There are at least two self-proclaimed capitals of the region, Paris and Mexico, but Fulton and Fayette have their supporters as well.

The notion of Little Dixie has also served as a stress-reducing agent, particularly for southerners during the bad days of Reconstruction, when a polished vision of a "little Dixie" helped lessen community and personal strain caused by the serious changes and adjustments that followed in the wake of the Confederacy's loss of the Civil War.

As an insider's region based on meaningful traditions and beliefs, the region exists. And the image flourishes quietly. It dwells in the expressive oral and material culture of Little Dixie and it dwells actively in the manipulation of this culture in newspaper stories and political speeches.

Little Dixie is a folk-cultural geographic region within the lower Midwest with composite midwestern features and at the same time special resemblances and kinships to its southern antecedents. Those patterns and tendencies join to produce a fascinating but elusive region. The limits of the area will shift and vary through time, but for now this definition seems to work: the region includes all of Boone, Howard, Randolph, Monroe, Audrain, Callaway, Pike, and Ralls counties, a tran-

Figure 6–4. Earl Westfall, traditional basketmaker, on his farm near Higbee, Howard County, 1969.

sitional zone fronting the Missouri River for several miles in Saline, Cooper, and Moniteau counties, the northern quarter of Cole County, the north and northwestern edges of Montgomery County, the north edge of Lincoln County, the southern and eastern quarters of Chariton County, and the southern quarters of Marion, Shelby, and Macon counties. That definition sounds clearer than it actually is. Exact dimensions of folk regions are impossible. And unnecessary.

Little Dixie has not become much more tangible for all this fuss. People will continue to be vague about its limits, and that is perfectly right. The regional theories that scholars cook up in seminar rooms are fine, but they falter when put to the test in conversations with people in everyday life. Internally, subjectively, Little Dixie is one's county and probably some sort of combination of neighboring counties or towns. Externally, objectively, based on the open and truthful documents that are material artifacts, Little Dixie certainly includes those eight counties listed above and a fuzzy-edged zone where patterns begin to vary. The fact is, politics is a tremendous force underpinning the Little Dixie notion, and the farmer's basic political and administrative unit—the county—is his region. What can be said now? Cultural regions are variable, complicated, and surprising when valid field documentation of real patterns is accomplished. And people's regions defy the standard scholarly approaches using set theories of regionalism. The depth and style of a region's personality will be different, if just a bit, the next time we pass that way.

Though this study is mainly architectural, the cultural context of traditional life and work on the land is inseparable. All our projects ought to commence with an understanding of the people and the local history that provide the living framework for the special topics we may pick out to concentrate on in our documentation and reporting.

For this region, Little Dixie, the combination of certain folk architectural features—especially the sort of log construction dominant and the prevalence of big I houses, little single-pen houses, and frame transverse-crib barns—powerfully shows how cultural expressions are carried over and transplanted in new settlement areas. Having solved the riddle of transplantation and provenience in earlier epochs, the greater riddles with useful messages for current historical revisions become how and in what ways traditional patterns of thought and work change over time and when conveyed into new landscapes and human environments. Little Dixie architecture is neither the simple replication of comfortable, known ideas and models nor some mighty creation of pioneer log civilization hacked out of the howling wilderness in the process of brute

Figure 6–5. Rocky Fork Church, Boone County.

Figure 6–6. Mr. and Mrs. Harold B. Schofield, near Hallsville, Boone County, 1974, and their fine Little Dixie I house.

survival. The alterations over time and the connections with Victorian fashion complicate the narrative but wonderfully increase its interest. From the perspective of this study, the study of buildings in traditional contexts does "afford the most direct and potent evidence of human cultures."[4] For the researcher interested in ordinary history and folk culture, architecture can be a fine guide to regional consciousness and identity and a sharp index to subtle, quiet cultural meanings.

When the words fade and others force the study and the theory further, the documentation of the folk architecture in this midwestern region will stand as a record of the vigorous ways people built shelter for life and work, a record of both their competence as thinkers and their performance as carpenters. And then the craft and memory of these people who lived their lives beyond the pages of formal history will have found their voice in the rhythmic chronicle of American civilization after all.

Notes

Notes to Preface

1. Henry Glassie, *Folk Housing in Middle Virginia: A Structural Analysis of Historic Artifacts*, pp. 17 ff.
2. See Iorwerth C. Peate, *Tradition and Folk Life: A Welsh View*, pp. 126–27, for a discussion of many researchers' initial emphases on rural life.
3. Henry Glassie, "Barns across Southern England: A Note on Transatlantic Comparisons and Architectural Meanings," p. 9.
4. In addition, other Little Dixies and plain Dixies have been identified in Oklahoma, Utah, and Texas.
5. "Discussion from the Floor," on Richard Dorson's paper, "A Theory for American Folklore."
6. Robert M. Crisler, "An Experiment in Regional Delimitation: The Little Dixie Region of Missouri," Ph.D. dissertation, Northwestern University, 1949; "Missouri's 'Little Dixie,'" *Missouri Historical Review* 42:2 (1948): 130–39; "The Regional Status of Little Dixie in Missouri and Little Egypt in Illinois," *Journal of Geography* 49:8 (1950): 337–43.
7. Albert Trombley, Columbia, 1922; Henry Belden, ed., *Ballads and Songs Collected by the Missouri Folk-Lore Society*; Robert L. Ramsay, *Our Storehouse of Missouri Place Names* (Columbia: University of Missouri Press, 1952); R. P. Christeson, *The Old-Time Fiddler's Repertory* (Columbia: University of Missouri Press, 1973).
8. The "preservation movement" is coming of age, and recent publications demonstrate a fresh and democratic spirit that bodes well; see Robert E. Stipe, ed., *New Directions in Rural Preservation* (Washington, D.C.: Heritage Conservation and Recreation Service, U.S. Department of Interior, 1980).
9. There are fine portraits of singers, tale tellers, and other people and pictures of material-culture features (johnboats, stills, a log house or two, a basketmaker riving out oak splits) in the "Vance Randolph Papers," Archive of Folksong Box 14, Library of Congress, Washington, D.C.; Randolph published a photograph of a saddle-notched log single-pen house in *Ozark Mountain Folks*, facing p. 126; several good folk houses are shown in Earl A. Collins, *Legends and Lore of Missouri*. None of these is a Little Dixie scene or subject.
10. In the direction of preservation, see Peter Smith, *Houses of the Welsh Countryside: A Study in Historical Geography*, pp. 328–31, and standard works like Charles B. Hosmer, Jr., *Presence of the Past: A History of the Preservation Movement in the United States before Williamsburg* (New York: G. P. Putnam's Sons, 1965); Orin M. Bullock, *The Restoration Manual* (Norwalk, Conn.: Atkin Productions, 1966); Harley J. McKee, *Recording Historic Buildings*; and three articles, Pierce Lewis, "The Future of the Past: Our Clouded Vision of Historic Preservation," *Pioneer America* 7:2 (July 1975): 1–20; David Lowenthal, "The American Scene," *Geographical Review* 58 (1968): 61–88; Howard Wight Marshall, "Folklife and the Rise of American Folk Museums," *Journal of American Folklore* 90:358 (October–December 1977): 391–413; and Thomas F. King, Patricia Hickmann, and Gary Berg, *Anthropology in Historic Preservation: Caring for Culture's Clutter* (New York: Academic Press, 1977).

Notes to Chapter 1

1. Albert E. Trombley, *Little Dixie*, p. 29, "Little Dixie."
2. James E. Collier, *Geographic Areas of Missouri* (Parkville, Mo.: 1959), pp. 4, 18; geographer Carl Ortwin Sauer wrote the best work on the Ozarks, *The Geography of the*

Ozark Highlands of Missouri, and folk-culture specialists know the Ozarks as Vance Randolph's domain. In Paul Nagel's *Missouri: A Bicentennial History*, p. 72, he lists Little Dixie as one of the state's six distinct regions (in addition to the Ozarks, Kansas City area, St. Louis area, the "bootheel" of southeast Missouri, and the vertical stack of counties of prairie farms along the Kansas border).

3. See Carl H. Chapman and Eleanor F. Chapman, *Indians and Archaeology of Missouri*, pp. 15, 26; and see various numbers of *The Missouri Archaeologist*. See also John R. Swanton, *Indian Tribes of North America*, and Francis La Flesche, "The Osage Tribe."

4. See Ellen Churchill Semple, *American History and Its Geographic Conditions*, p. 100, and Walter Williams, *A History of Northeast Missouri*, 1:15.

5. Eilleen Trimble Fleming, "Missouri's Religious Heritage," in Howard Wight Marshall, ed., *Old Families of Randolph County, Missouri: A People's History*, p. 36.

6. See Frederick Simpich, "These Missourians," *National Geographic* 89:3 (March 1946): 279. Robert L. Ramsay, *Our Storehouse of Missouri Place Names* (Columbia: University of Missouri Press, 1952), pp. 21–22; of the place names within Little Dixie, Ramsay's compilation shows that all of the counties are named for southern places, immigrants, or national figures with southern or local associations.

7. Dan Elbert Clark, *The Middle West in American History*, p. 188, and Thomas D. Clark, *Frontier America*, pp. 307–8; C. R. Burns, ed., *Switzler's Illustrated History of Missouri from 1541 to 1877*, pp. 177–97 (including a discussion of "Boone's Lick country" as the earliest local name for central Missouri, p. 197), and Nagel, *Missouri*, p. 76; Russell L. Gerlach emphasizes the importance of Kentuckians and Virginians in central Missouri settlement in "Population Origins in Rural Missouri," *Missouri Historical Review* 71:1 (October 1976): 1–21.

8. William A. Foley, *A History of Missouri, Volume I: 1673–1820* (Columbia: University of Missouri Press, 1971), pp. 40, 46, 52, 164–66. See also Ward Dorrance's outstanding *The Survival of French in the Old District of Sainte Genevieve*, and Eugene M. Violette, *A History of Missouri*, p. 74.

9. Interview with Bill and Mary B. Creson, farm near Yates, Howard County, June 1972; interview with Mrs. Frances J. Marshall, Moberly, Randolph County, June 1975.

10. In a new history of the state, Nagel acknowledges Little Dixie's place as a genuine region of the state and suggests its importance in politics and the development of Missouri's personality. *Missouri*, pp. 16, 76–90.

11. Among the best county histories are Alexander H. Waller, *History of Randolph County, Missouri*; *History of Monroe and Shelby Counties, Missouri . . .* ; and *History of Callaway County, Missouri . . .* ; such local histories are a source of family history and all sorts of informal cultural information; and see Marshall, ed., *Old Families of Randolph County*, in which I published family and local histories as written by the people themselves.

In addition, there are other excellent books written years ago. See Richard M. Dorson, *American Folklore and the Historian* (Chicago: University of Chicago Press, 1972), p. 119; good examples are John Josselyn and Frederick Law Olmsted, but Henry Adams pointed to the precariousness of travel accounts in 1889 in *The United States in 1800*, p. 30. The best bile is still the observations of Mrs. Frances Trollope, "a bustling and bonneted little lawyer's wife with sharp, observant eyes and a sharp tongue" who visited in America in 1827 (see Russell Lynes, *The Tastemakers*, p. 5).

12. Waller, *History of Randolph County*, pp. 147–66, breaks the population down by townships; "Nearly all of the above pioneers were from Kentucky and many of these men were great hunters [Prairie Township]." And see Marshall, *Old Families of Randolph County*, the section titled "Centennial Farms," in which twenty-two of the twenty-seven centennial farms (farms owned by the same family for at least one hundred years) were settled by Kentuckians, Virginians, or North Carolinians (pp. 421–92).

13. Charles Joseph Latrobe, *Rambles in North America, 1832–1833*, p. 121; and see Herschel Tupes, "The Influence of Slavery upon Missouri Politics (to Include 1860)," p. 3; we could develop a chart based on this work to show the dominance of

southern immigrants in the state overall—again, Kentucky leads, followed by Virginia, Tennessee, and North Carolina (p. 93).

14. See Charles van Ravenswaay, *The Arts and Architecture of German Settlements in Missouri: A Survey of a Vanishing Culture*, especially the introduction and chapter one.

15. Interview with Bill and Mary B. Creson; interview with John Wells, Fulton, Callaway County, August 1974; interview with Clarence L. Klink, Huntsville, Randolph County, August 1974.

16. Violette, *History of Missouri*, p. 381; papaws are edible for only a brief time in season. James A. Hamilton, in "The Enrolled Missouri Militia: Its Creation and Controversial History," tries to improve the image of the "Paw Paw militia" (actually the 81st and 83d Regiments, Enrolled Missouri Militia) and offers an equally good reason for the nickname: "These units are believed to have received this nickname from the Paw Paw bushes in the Missouri River bottoms in Platte and Clay counties or for their propensity to hide 'in the bushes' with the guerrillas when not on duty" (pp. 427–28).

17. John C. Crighton, "Many Facets Contributed to Seething Unrest," *Columbia Daily Tribune*, Boone County history series, August 1974. The bushwhackers did not always go unpunished; Union General Merrill ordered eleven federal militiamen hanged near Macon in 1862, after the robbery and murder of some neighbors (Floyd C. Shoemaker, ed., *Missouri Day by Day*, 2:204–5).

18. Richard S. Brownlee, *Grey Ghosts of the Confederacy: Guerilla Warfare in the West, 1861–1865*, is a good treatment of the subject; about the tintype of one such rebel yahoo, I was told, "He was just some relative—I don't know anything about him or his name. Dad said he was a 'no-good' and that he rode with Anderson's gang" (F. J. Marshall, Moberly, Randolph County, May 1974). Also see Burns, *Switzler's Illustrated History*, p. 438, and Nagel, *Missouri*, p. 134.

19. Violette, *History of Missouri*, p. 291; both "sold down South" and "sold down the river" (meaning the Mississippi or the Missouri River to St. Louis) are still in circulation and are used to denote betrayal of a friendship or agreement.

20. Tupes, "Influence of Slavery," p. 15; Kenneth M. Stampp, *The Peculiar Institution*, pp. 30, 138.

21. State Historical Society of Missouri, comp., *Historic Missouri*, pp. 33, 34; Lew Larkin, *Vanguard of Empire: Missouri's Century of Expansion*, p. 248.·

22. For example, Carl Wittke's *We Who Built America: The Saga of the Immigrant* contains slanted accounts illuminating the brooding antagonisms between German farmers and their neighbors. Mr. Clarence L. Klink of Huntsville is descended from German immigrants: "Grandpaw came here from Bavaria before the [Civil] war. He didn't fight though—he paid for a man to fight in his place. . . . He run off from Germany. His sister smuggled him out at the age of fourteen, to escape the army. Y'know, there was a high class o' Germans and there was a low class o' Germans in them days—and the low class ruled the country, you know, like Hitler, and they ruined things. . . . He landed in New York in 1830. He was a baker by trade. Then he drifted west to Missouri pretty soon after." Miss Martha Teupker, Mexico, Audrain County, August 1974: "We found it difficult, even though we spoke English. We were very frugal. It was hard for us to borrow money. The English people didn't accept us very readily until we proved ourselves. But as the years went by, the Germans kept the land in the families, while the English lost their land in the Depression. . . . The Germans have a way of buckling down—they're hardworking. They had their own churches, and the preaching was in German till World War One came along and it was outlawed." See van Ravenswaay, *Arts and Architecture*.

23. Wittke, *We Who Built America*, pp. 204–5; and see van Ravenswaay, *Arts and Architecture*.

24. James T. Lemon, *The Best Poor Man's Country: A Geographical Study of Early Southeastern Pennsylvania*, p. 85.

25. van Ravenswaay, *Arts and Architecture*, pp. 8, 14: "Without the friendly aid of these American neighbors, it is unlikely that many German settlements could have survived, or that they could have succeeded so well and relatively quickly."

26. Robert M. Crisler, "An Experiment in Regional Delimitation: The Little Dixie Region of Missouri" (Ph.D. diss., Northwestern University, 1949), p. 46; Robert M. Crisler, "Missouri's 'Little Dixie,'" *Missouri Historical Review* 42:2 (1948): 130–39.

27. State Historical Society of Missouri, comp., *Historic Missouri*, p. 18. For a good treatment of the ways politicians use past glories and images of the good old days see Richard Hofstader, *The American Political Tradition* (1948), quoted in Alan Gowans, *Images of American Living: Four Centuries of Architecture and Furniture as Cultural Expression*, p. 364; and see W. J. Cash, *The Mind of the South* (New York: Alfred A. Knopf, 1941), p. 132, a well-known treatment of the rise of the Democratic party, which effectively encouraged a one-party system in the Deep South. If comparisons between Little Dixie politics and the bigger Dixie are drawn, the soundest statement would be simply that both places favor the Democratic party, and that it has prevailed since Reconstruction.

Notes to Chapter 2

1. This inclusive definition was made into government policy in The American Folklife Preservation Act (Public Law 94–201, January 1976), which provides the legislative mandate for the American Folklife Center at the Library of Congress in Washington, D.C., the designated agency to preserve and present American folk culture through leadership in the discipline, assistance, and experimental projects. There are many definitions of folklife in the literature that encompass the more familiar idea of "folklore"; see, for example, Sigurd Erixon, "An Introduction to Folklife Research or Nordic Ethnology," p. 5; Ake Hultkrantz, *General Ethnological Concepts* (Copenhagen: Rosenkilde and Bagger, 1960), p. 133; Iorwerth C. Peate, *Tradition and Folk Life: A Welsh View*, pp. 18–20; Don Yoder, "The Folklife Studies Movement"; Don Yoder, "Folklife Studies in American Scholarship" in his *American Folklife* (Austin: University of Texas Press, 1976), pp. 3–18; and Richard M. Dorson's introduction to his *Folklore and Folklife: An Introduction*, pp. 1–50. In Europe, where folklife research began in the nineteenth century, terms of contemporary usage in addition to *folklife* include *vie populaire*, *Volksleben*, *vida popular*, *folkliv*, and due to the stress on regions, *regional ethnology*. Our sense of folklife comes mainly from Scandinavia and Britain.

2. James Deetz, "Material Culture and Archaeology—What's the Difference?," in Leland Ferguson, ed., *Historical Archaeology and the Importance of Material Things*, p. 10; readers can become acquainted with Deetz and with Glassie's seminal material culture writings in: James Deetz, *Invitation to Archaeology*, and Henry Glassie, *Pattern in the Material Folk Culture of the Eastern United States*; their recent explorations are boldest in James Deetz, *In Small Things Forgotten: The Archaeology of Early American Life*, and Henry Glassie, *Folk Housing in Middle Virginia: A Structural Analysis of Historic Artifacts*.

3. Cary Carson, "The 'Virginia House' in Maryland," p. 185.

4. None of the dictionaries has an entry for folk architecture, nor does the valuable *Funk and Wagnalls Standard Dictionary of Folklore, Mythology, and Legend*, ed. Maria Leach (New York: Funk and Wagnalls, 1972); the extraordinary range of publications considered inside the realm of "folk architecture" is shown in the diversity of a recent bibliography, Howard Wight Marshall, *American Folk Architecture: A Selected Bibliography*.

5. See George Kubler, *The Shape of Time: Remarks on the Hstory of Things*, for effective discussion of the need for—and the lack of—categories of art.

6. Michael Southern, "The I House as a Carrier of Style in Three Counties of the Northeast Piedmont" in Doug Swaim, ed., *Carolina Dwelling*, p. 70 (author Southern does not disapprove). In a personal communication, Carl W. Condit summarized style: "What we call style in the true sense is an intricate symbolic reconstruction of some kind of encompassing order" (13 November 1978).

7. Ake Campbell, "Notes on the Irish House," *Folk-Liv* 1 (1937): 207–34; 2 (1938): 173–96.

8. Condit personal communication, November 1978.

9. As it was in an influential chestnut by Fred Kniffen and Henry Glassie, "Building in Wood in the Eastern United States: A Time-Place Perspective," and throughout Glassie's *Pattern in the Material Folk Culture*, which is essentially a classic historic–geographic study in its methodology.

10. See Pierce F. Lewis, "Common Houses, Cultural Spoor"; John Fraser Hart, *The Look of the Land*; Glassie, *Pattern in the Material Folk Culture*; Fred B. Kniffen, "Folk Housing: Key to Diffusion"; Iorwerth C. Peate, *The Welsh House: A Study in Folk Culture*; E. Estyn Evans, *Irish Folk Ways* and *Mourne Country: Landscape and Life in South Down*; Ronald W. Brunskill, *Illustrated Handbook of Vernacular Architecture*; Wilbur Zelinsky, *The Cultural Geography of the United States*; Abbott Lowell Cummings, *The Framed Houses of Massachusetts Bay, 1625–1725*; G. H. Riviere, "Folk Architecture—Past, Present, and Future"; Swaim, *Carolina Dwelling*; and Alec Clifton-Taylor, *The Pattern of English Building*.

11. For important and differing approaches see Amos Rapoport and Christopher Alexander, *Notes on the Synthesis of Form*; Deetz, *In Small Things Forgotten*; Glassie, *Folk Housing in Middle Virginia*; Christian Norberg-Schulz, *Intentions in Architecture*; Kubler, *The Shape of Time*; Russell Lynes, *The Tastemakers*; Robert Venturi, Denise Scott Brown, and Steven Izenour, *Learning from Las Vegas: The Forgotten Symbolism of Architectural Form* (Cambridge: M.I.T. Press, 1977).

12. Christopher Williams, "Craftsmen of Necessity," *Natural History* 89:1 (November 1972): 48–59. See also Alan Gowans, *Images of American Living: Four Centuries of Architecture and Furniture as Cultural Expression*, p. 16, and "The Unselfconscious Process" in Alexander, *Notes*, pp. 46–54.

13. Alexander, *Notes*, p. 15, and see Glassie, *Folk Housing in Middle Virginia*, pp. 119–20.

14. The clearest and most important discussion of form, construction, and use (which Norberg-Schulz calls "form, technics, and use") is by Glassie in *Pattern in the Material Folk Culture*, pp. 7–12; some researchers have thought style ("decoration" or "cosmetic features") to be more important than use in this threefold delineation—as in Bernard L. Herman and David G. Orr, "Pear Valley et al.: An Excursion into the Analysis of Southern Vernacular Architecture," and Gerald L. Pocius, *Textile Traditions of Eastern Newfoundland* (Ottawa: National Museum of Man, Canadian Centre for Folk Culture Studies, Paper No. 29, 1979), pp. 55–66. All four ingredients should be studied (form, construction, use, and decoration).

15. Glassie's massive paper on barns, "The Variation of Concepts within Tradition: Barn Building in Otsego County, New York," is a tour de force on techniques and the ways people vary what seem to be very rigid traditional patterns.

16. Among the possibilities, see Deetz, *In Small Things Forgotten*, pp. 111–17; Glassie, *Pattern in the Material Folk Culture* and *Folk Housing in Middle Virginia*; Hugh Braun, *A Short History of English Architecture* (London: Faber and Faber, 1950), pp. 160–72; Ronald Brunskill, *Vernacular Architecture of the Lake Counties*; and Clifton-Taylor, *Pattern of English Building*.

17. Henry Glassie, "Folk Art," in Richard M. Dorson, ed., *Folklore and Folklife: An Introduction*, p. 274.

18. There are numerous guides to fieldwork in the humanities and in the social sciences; for useful introductions and very different approaches, see Ray Birdwhistell, *Kinesics and Context* (Philadelphia: University of Pennsylvania Press, 1970); Ronald W. Brunskill, "A Systematic Procedure for Recording English Vernacular Architecture"; John Collier, Jr., *Visual Anthropology: Photography as a Research Method* (New York: Holt, Rinehart and Winston, 1967); Holly Cutting-Baker, et al., *Family Folklore* (Washington, D.C.: Smithsonian Institution Folklife Programs, 1976); Kenneth S. Goldstein, *A Guide for Field Workers in Folklore* (Hatboro, Pa.: Folklore Associates, 1964); David Greenhood, *Mapping* (Chicago: University of Chicago Press, 1951); J. W. Y. Higgs, *Folk Life Collection and Classification*; W. G. Hoskins, *Fieldwork in Local History*; Edward D. Ives,

A Manual for Field Workers (Orono, Me.: Northeast Folklore Society, 1974); McEdward Leach and Henry Glassie, *A Guide for Collectors of Oral Traditions and Folk Cultural Materials in Pennsylvania*; Harley J. McKee, comp., *Recording Historic Buildings*; Thomas B. Renk, "A Guide to Recording Structural Details of Historic Buildings," *Historical Archaeology* 3 (1969): 34–48; Warren E. Roberts, "Fieldwork: Recording Material Culture," in Dorson, ed., *Folklore and Folklife*, pp. 431–44; James Spradley and D. W. McCurdy, *The Cultural Experience: Ethnography in Complex Society* (Chicago: Science Research Associates, 1972); William C. Sturtevant, *Guide to Field Collecting of Ethnographic Specimens*; Thomas Rhys Williams, *Field Methods in the Study of Culture* (New York: Holt, Rinehart and Winston, 1967); a productive general statement for the layman is Peter Bartis, *Folklife and Fieldwork* (Washington, D.C.: Publications of the American Folklife Center No. 3, 1979); and Sean O'Sullivan's massive and suggestive *A Handbook of Irish Folklore* (1942. Reprint, Detroit: Singing Tree Press, 1970).

Notes to Chapter 3

1. Alan Gowans, *Images of American Living: Four Centuries of Architecture and Furniture as Cultural Expression*, p. 14; Henry Glassie, *Folk Housing in Middle Virginia: A Structural Analysis of Historic Artifacts* and *Pattern in the Material Folk Culture of the Eastern United States*, p. 34 (regions are not "isolated pockets"); R. P. Christeson's *The Old-Time Fiddler's Repertory* (Columbia: University of Missouri Press, 1975) includes many nineteenth-century central Missouri tunes of "midwestern" character that are regional versions of older southern ones.

2. John Fraser Hart, *The Look of the Land*, pp. 155–56; Pierce F. Lewis, "Common Houses, Cultural Spoor," p. 3; the classic treatment of the movement of architectural traditions is Fred Kniffen's "Folk Housing: Key to Diffusion"; Charles van Ravenswaay's *The Arts and Architecture of German Settlements in Missouri: A Survey of a Vanishing Culture* is a model study of "ethnic" material culture that is regional as well.

3. Lewis, "Common Houses," pp. 1–3, 10; Bruce Allsopp, *The Study of Architectural History* (London: Studio Vista, 1970), p. 97; and Glassie, *Folk Housing in Middle Virginia*, a complex and fascinating treatise on folk houses in terms of structuralist theory (from Claude Lévi-Strauss mainly) and generative grammar (from Noam Chomsky mainly), explaining how houses in Goochland and Louisa counties are based on an intricate language of patterns with the English square single-pen house as the elemental unit, and how builders in Virginia imposed order in their lives (by changing their architecture) in an age of political, social, and economic troubles. In this wide-ranging study, Glassie describes what he sees as historians' shortcomings (due to "unexplained process," elitism, and "unscientific procedure"), pp. 8–9.

4. See H. G. Barnett, *Innovation: The Basis of Cultural Change*, for a basic work; for architecture, see Henry Glassie, "The Variation of Concepts within Tradition: Barn-Building in Otsego County, New York"; and J. T. Smith, "The Evolution of the English Peasant House to the Late Seventeenth Century: The Evidence of the Buildings."

5. Glassie, *Pattern in the Material Folk Culture*, pp. 3, 8–12 (architectural floorplans are stable and do "not depend on oral transmission or mutation" for their preservation); form (floorplan) lasts after original function changes and after new uses are found for buildings now obsolete (pp. 7–9); Amos Rapoport also urges attention to floorplan in *House Form and Culture*, as does Wilbur Zelinsky in *The Cultural Geography of the United States*, p. 74 ("house design, which might seem wholly technological . . . is . . . associated with the nature of family and social system and so also with religious or cosmological ideas"); and see Carl Ortwin Sauer, "Foreword to Historical Geography," *Annals of the Association of American Geographers* 31 (1941): 21.

6. Standard arguments for and examples of fieldwork concentrating on floorplans and construction include J. Geraint Jenkins, "Field-Work and Documentation in Folk-Life Studies"; Iorwerth C. Peate, *The Welsh House: A Study in Folk Culture*; Sir Cyril Fox and Lord Raglan, *Monmouthshire Houses: A Study of Building Techniques and Smaller*

House-Plans in the Fifteenth to Seventeenth Centuries; M. W. Barley, *The English Farmhouse and Cottage*; Ronald W. Brunskill, *Illustrated Handbook of Vernacular Architecture* and *Vernacular Architecture of the Lake Counties*; Warren E. Roberts, "Recording Material Culture" in Richard M. Dorson, ed., *Folklore and Folklife: An Introduction*; Glassie, *Pattern in the Material Folk Culture* and *Folk Housing in Middle Virginia*; Eric Mercer, *English Vernacular Houses: A Study of Traditional Farmhouses and Cottages*; Peter Smith, *Houses of the Welsh Countryside*; Fred Kniffen, "Louisiana House Types"; Abbott Lowell Cummings, *The Framed Houses of Massachusetts Bay, 1625–1725*.

7. See Henry Glassie, "The Types of the Southern Mountain Cabin," pp. 338–70, and *Pattern in the Material Folk Culture*, pp. 195 ff., for information on certain antecedents to Little Dixie architecture; for antecedents of the Germanic building in Little Dixie, see van Ravenswaay, *Arts and Architecture*, part 2 ("Buildings"); though not particularly relevant to Little Dixie, chapter 1 ("The English Background") in Cummings, *Framed Houses of Massachusetts Bay*, is a model of good historical background research.

8. Folk-house "types" acquire formal names in various and mysterious ways; some like "double pen," "saddlebag," "dogtrot," and "single pen" (also called "cabin") come from traditional usage by builders and users, and some, like "central-hall house," "I house" (so named by geographer Fred Kniffen after years of studying them in Indiana, Illinois, and Iowa and partly because from a certain standpoint the version with tall end chimneys resembles a capital *I*), "stack house" (two single-pen houses stacked up tall, which I named in 1974), and "hall-and-parlor house" come from researchers' attempts to clarify terminology (seldom successful, but house "types" need names).

9. Glassie, *Pattern in the Material Folk Culture*, pp. 88, 89.

10. Henry Glassie, "The Double-Crib Barn in South Central Pennsylvania." The double-crib barn diffused from its Pennsylvania source area throughout the southern mountains and thus into the lower Midwest; see Henry Glassie, "The Pennsylvania Barn in the South" and "The Old Barns of Appalachia."

11. Architectural historian Edward Chappell produced a thesis at the University of Virginia, "Cultural Change in the Shenandoah Valley: Northern Augusta County Houses" (1977), documenting the combination of British and English houses with German agricultural buildings; I have documented similar scenes of American and German interaction in Indiana; and see van Ravenswaay, *Arts and Architecture*, pp. 7–19.

12. Rexford Newcomb, *Old Kentucky Architecture*, introduction; James C. Thomas, "The Log Houses of Kentucky," *The Magazine Antiques* 105:4 (1974): 792–96. C. Lancaster, *Ante Bellum Houses of the Bluegrass*, has a fine chapter on "Pioneer Building," and he breaks log construction into two phases (p. 2): "primitive" log houses with unseasoned round logs, dirt or puncheon (halved log) floors, and cat-and-clay chimneys, and an advanced log-building stage of hewn seasoned timbers and a more "finished-looking and workmanlike" result. William Lynwood Montell and Michael Lynn Morse, *Kentucky Folk Architecture* (Lexington: University Press of Kentucky, 1976).

13. The village was at one time considered a potential location for the state capital; I helped survey Woodland Indian burial mounds there for the Missouri State Park Board; and see C. Johnson, "Missouri-French Houses: Some Relict Features in Missouri," and Ward A. Dorrance, *The Survival of French in the Old District of Sainte Genevieve*.

14. See Kniffen, "Louisiana House Types"; Milton B. Newton, Jr., "Louisiana House Types: A Field Guide," *Melanges* 2 (September 1971); Eugene M. Wilson, *Alabama Folk Houses*; Julia Cook Guice, *The Buildings of Biloxi: An Architectural Survey* (Mississippi: City of Biloxi, 1976); John Michael Vlach, "The Shotgun House: An Africal Architectural Legacy," *Pioneer America* 8:1 (January 1976): 47–56 and 8:2 (July 1976): 57–70; Frederick Doveton Nichols, *The Architecture of Georgia* (Chapel Hill: University of North Carolina Press, 1957); Patti Carr Black, *Mississippi Woods: A Photographic Study of Folk Architecture* (Jackson: Mississippi Department of Archives and History, 1976).

Diane Tebbetts recorded the range of house types in north-central Arkansas and sorted out six types—single-pen houses, double-pen houses, dogtrot houses, central-hall houses, saddlebag houses, and I houses—that, although similar in kind, differ in technical execution; "Traditional Houses of Independence County, Arkansas"; more productive, of course, are studies of building in sections of Virginia and Kentucky where Little Dixie people actually migrated from. Certain studies of Tennessee and North Carolina houses are very helpful, too (though lesser in settlement importance); see Edna Schofield, "The Evolution and Development of Tennessee Houses"; Norbert F. Riedl, Donald B. Ball, and Anthony P. Cavender, *A Survey of Traditional Architecture and Related Material Folk Culture Patterns in the Normandy Reservoir, Coffee County, Tennessee*; Doug Swaim, ed., *Carolina Dwelling*; Frances Benjamin Johnston and Thomas Tileston Waterman, *The Early Architecture of North Carolina*.

15. van Ravenswaay, *Arts and Architecture*; Terry G. Jordan, *Texas Log Buildings: A Folk Architecture*; and see Hubert G. H. Wilhelm, "German Settlement and Building Practices in the Hill Country of Texas," *Pioneer America* 3:2 (July 1971): 15–24; Germans in Texas used stone and mortar to fill in half-timbered walls; see also Hubert G. H. Wilhelm and Michael Miller, "Half-Timber Construction: A Relic Building Method in Ohio"; and William J. Murtagh, "Half-Timbering in American Architecture," describes the tradition's frequency in Germany (as van Ravenswaay does), but also its frequency in England.

16. There are five different terms used for the T house, suggesting the lack of attention that has been paid to dwelling type by scholars (and their lack of agreement on what to call things they study): T house; "upright-and-wing house," used by Pierce F. Lewis to describe these "architectural fossils" left by New Englanders (in "Common Houses, Cultural Spoor," p. 15); "temple-form house," used by Glassie in *Pattern in the Material Folk Culture*, p. 129, stressing the door in the gable end and the low wing or wings and thinking of the houses as a "nonfolk, Greek Revival form" that became dominant in the North and across the upper Midwest; "cross-wing house," used by R. C. Watson for seventeenth-century stone examples in Lancashire, England, in "Parlours with External Entrances," *Vernacular Architecture* 6 (1975): 28–32; and "L-house."

17. Glassie, *Pattern in the Material Folk Culture*, *Folk Housing in Middle Virginia*, and "The Types of the Southern Mountain Cabin"; for Kentucky, see Montell and Morse, *Kentucky Folk Architecture*. The single-pen house is common across the Carolinas as well as in Virginia and Kentucky; see Swaim, "North Carolina Folk Housing," in *Carolina Dwelling*, p. 30.

18. Charles A. Weslager, *The Log Cabin in America*, p. 34, shows a log single-pen house near Ashland (Boone County), a V-notched square house with "no windows or chimney"; it likely had had a brick stove chimney that fell or was taken down when the house was vacated. Weslager was told that its date of construction is 1810, but that seems early. In this book, unless otherwise noted, houses are measured by inside dimensions and barns by outside (in linear feet, the way they were built); dimensions are usually for the core of the building only, not additions.

19. For example, see E. A. Collins and Albert F. Elsea, *Missouri, Its People and Its Progress*, pp. 29–30; Henry Rowe Schoolcraft, *Journal of a Tour into the Interior of Missouri and Arkansaw . . .* , pp. 30, 31, 36; J. M. Peck, *A Guide for Emigrants, Containing Sketches of Illinois, Missouri . . .* (Boston, 1831), p. 126; and Reuben Gold Thwaites, *Early Western Travels, 1748–1846 . . .* , 14:134–35.

20. For the basic building block, see Glassie, *Folk Housing in Middle Virginia*; Mercer, *English Vernacular Houses*, p. 2; and Peter Smith, *Houses of the Welsh Countryside: A Study in Historical Geography*, pp. 164–65—"The minimum house consisted of a hall . . . with a chamber above." For information on expanding single-pen houses, see Glassie, *Pattern in the Material Folk Culture*, "The Types of the Southern Mountain Cabin," and *Folk Housing in Middle Virginia*; Cummings, *Framed Houses of Massachusetts Bay*. A fine V-notched log single-pen house was discovered inside an expanded house when demolition was beginning; see Orville Sittler, "Little House on Prairie Resurrected by Strada," *Moberly Monitor-Index and Evening Democrat*, 22 October 1978; the house, dat-

ing from early Kentucky settlers in Little Dixie, was saved by the builder's great-great-grandson. Another house type, the hall-and-parlor house, also developed from the single-pen house; see Glassie, *Pattern in the Material Folk Culture*, pp. 64–66, 80–81, and Cary Carson, "The 'Virginia House' in Maryland," for Holly Hill in eighteenth-century Maryland. A similar system of subdividing and extending occurs in every Euro-pean-American folk-housing configuration; for eighteenth-century Irish examples that are antecedents for American and Little Dixie ones, see Alan Gailey, "Some Develop-ments and Adaptations of Traditional House Types," in Kevin Danaher, ed., *Folk and Farm: Essays in Honor of A. T. Lucas* (Dublin: Royal Society of Antiquaries of Ireland, 1976), pp. 40–53.

21. The excellently functional open central hallway that became a regular feature of the dwelling in the Deep South illustrates how folk-building design answers human needs; see Howard Wight Marshall, "Dogtrot Comfort: A Note on Traditional Houses and Energy Efficiency"; the article includes examples in Missouri's Little Dixie and Geor-gia's "wiregrass" regions.

22. Thwaites, *Early Western Travels*, pp. 134–45. Like the transverse-crib barn, the dogtrot house is not a standard part of the configuration in the oldest British and Chesapeake Tidewater and Piedmont source areas; it was added to the pack in the Ten-nessee and Kentucky stopovers.

23. Samuel Langhorne Clemens, *Adventures of Huckleberry Finn* (Scranton, Pa.: Chandler Facsimile edition of 1885 original, 1962), p. 142; unfortunately illustrator E. J. Kemble (a gifted engraver and artist) presents a misleading picture of the Granger-fords' house. Earlier, Clemens described Huck's Pap's rough log "cabin," a single-pen house of the early variety (which illustrator Kemble renders nicely on p. 54). Some present-day Monroe County residents know the old farms and buildings that were the basis for Clemens's fiction—the sort of fiction that through its glowing detailing of everyday life gives us more of the heart of Little Dixie than any history book can.

24. As described by Glassie in a tantalizing footnote that interested me in figuring out this house type, from "The Types of the Southern Mountain Cabin," p. 364: "There are two-story one room houses in the Southern Mountains; these have floorplans of the same proportions as the cabins but usually have larger dimensions." For published ex-amples of stack houses, see Glassie, *Folk Housing in Middle Virginia*, pp. 81, 82–84; Tebbetts, "Traditional Houses of Independence County," p. 45; Montell and Morse, *Kentucky Folk Architecture*, p. 30; and Peter O. Wacker, *The Musconetcong Valley of New Jersey: A Historical Geography*, pp. 88–89, 148–51, for his "small East Jersey cottage," which is the stack-house type. I have recorded stack houses in Virginia's Tidewater and Piedmont, in Piedmont North Carolina, and in southern Indiana. Brunskill documented a good English example (which he calls a "one up and one down cottage") in *Vernacular Architecture of the Lake Counties*, p. 70. I coined the term.

25. Classic definitions of the I-house type (Glassie, *Pattern in the Material Folk Culture*, p. 49, and elsewhere) require two full stories, which I amend to include houses only one and a half stories tall of certain quality if other ingredients are there. For an example of the antecedents to this kind of house in Britain (its real source area), there is a photograph of a stone version "thoroughly in the Scottish tradition" on the Island of Barra, in Michael Barley, *The House and Home: A Review of 900 Years of House Planning and Furnishing in Great Britain*, pl. 226. This apparently typical Scottish farmhouse, if of wooden construction, would be right at home in Little Dixie. For an example of English antecedents, see Brunskill, *Illustrated Handbook*, p. 108, where Example C shows a cross section of a one-and-a-half-story house with dormer windows and raised main hall that is like the Scottish and Little Dixie examples. Other examples abound in the literature on British and American "domestic" and "vernacular" architecture. The term *I house* was coined by cultural geographer Fred Kniffen, who identified and analyzed the type mainly in Indiana, Illinois, and Iowa years ago; Glassie, Kniffen, and others have noted the transplantation of I houses to the Midwest from the upper South where they

typify many areas. See, for example, Lewis, "Common Houses, Cultural Spoor," p. 10, and Howard Wight Marshall and John Michael Vlach, "Toward a Folklife Approach to American Dialects." What is early for Little Dixie, though (1820), is late for the appearance of the house type itself, which in England and Britain was built well before 1700. See, among others, Barley, *The House and Home*, fig. 130 for a 1713 Scottish example. "Bacon's Castle" in Surry County, Virginia, dating from 1655, is in plan a fancy Jacobean-styled version of an I house; see Gowans, *Images of American Living*, p. 105. Central-chimney I houses were built in early New England, too; see Cummings, *Framed Houses of Massachusetts Bay*, pp. 23–27, for three fine examples. I houses are rare in the Deep South in my own field experience (I recorded only one in an eight-county survey in south Georgia in 1977).

26. The central-hall I house (built of walnut logs and weatherboarded at once) built by Captain Wight and his family, completed about 1840, is located between Milton and Madison in Randolph County and once was the center of a considerable agricultural domain.

27. See Glassie, *Pattern in the Material Folk Culture*, p. 184; I tend to agree with those who argue that too much is made of the influence of local climate on the shapes and techniques of folk houses in history.

28. Ibid., p. 99, and Kniffen, "Folk Housing," p. 55; see also John Maass, *Victorian Architecture: Two Pattern Books by A. J. Bicknell and William T. Comstock* (Watkins Glen, N.Y.: American Life Foundation, 1970), introduction, for a good discussion of the desire for "fine houses" in the nineteenth century; James O'Malley points to I houses as "an indicator of agricultural opulence" in "Functional Aspects of Folk Housing: A Case for the 'I' House, Union County, Tennessee," *Tennessee Folklore Society Bulletin* 38 (1972): 1–4.

29. Interview with John D. Williams, farm near Fayette, Howard County; Mr. Williams is the great-great-grandson of the builder, Colden Williams, a Revolutionary War veteran; a kitchen ell addition (in the form of a log saddlebag house) was added to the big house between 1820 and 1825.

Notes to Chapter 4

1. For discussions of the transverse-crib barn, see Fred Kniffen, "Folk Housing: Key to Diffusion," p. 566, and Henry Glassie, *Pattern in the Material Folk Culture of the Eastern United States*, pp. 88–93, 157; in *The Look of the Land*, p. 133, geographer John Fraser Hart says that the transverse-crib type and the "general purpose barn or feeder barn" are the most significant midwestern types, an assertion logical for the upper Midwest but not for the lower Midwest, which contains regions like Little Dixie and southern Indiana.

2. Charles van Ravenswaay, *The Arts and Architecture of German Settlements in Missouri: A Survey of a Vanishing Culture*, p. 264; the generalizations about Germans as more careful planners and carpenters than their Anglo-American neighbors need considerable testing.

3. van Ravenswaay, *Arts and Architecture*, p. 268.

4. The traditions of smokehouse building, and of keeping meat, were discussed in Howard Wight Marshall, "Meat Preservation on the Farm in Missouri's Little Dixie"; the floorplans in Figure 4–13 were included in the article.

Notes to Chapter 5

1. Robert P. Multhauf, "America's Wooden Age," in Charles E. Peterson, ed., *Building Early America* (Radnor, Pa.: Chilton Book Company, 1976), p. 23, and see Brooke Hindle, *America's Wooden Age: Aspects of Its Early Technology* (Tarrytown, N.Y.: Sleepy Hollow Restorations, 1976); the work to consult is Fred B. Kniffen and Henry Glassie, "Building in Wood in the Eastern United States: A Time-Place Perspective."

2. See Warren E. Roberts, "The Tools Used in Building Log Houses in Indiana," *Pioneer America* 9:1 (July 1977): 30–61.

3. See Kniffen and Glassie, "Building in Wood," p. 41.

4. In British and Anglo-American folk building, timber was the first choice, and stone and brick came to popularity when the great forests began to be depleted and worn out; see Iorwerth C. Peate, *The Welsh House: A Study in Folk Culture*, pp. 21, 30 ff. See also Trudy West, *The Timber-Frame House in England* (Newton Abbot, Eng.: David and Charles, 1971), pp. 13 ff., and Sidney Oldall Addy, *Evolution of English House*, p. 228.

5. Peter C. Marzio, "Carpentry in the Southern Colonies during the Eighteenth Century with Emphasis on Maryland and Virginia," p. 246.

6. Andrew Jackson Downing, *The Architecture of Country Houses*, pp. 76–77.

7. Russell Lynes, *The Tastemakers*, p. 109, and see Kniffen and Glassie, "Building in Wood," and James Marston Fitch, *American Building*; for an important discussion of the ancient box-framing methods prefiguring balloon framing, see J. T. Smith, "Timber-Framed Building in England: Its Development and Regional Differences," *Archaeological Journal* 122 (1965), and Cecil Alex Hewitt, *The Development of Carpentry, 1200–1700: An Essex Study* (New York: Augustus M. Kelley, 1969).

8. Kniffen and Glassie, "Building in Wood," p. 48.

9. Like many contemporary researchers, architectural historian Judith Kitchen blasts the "myths" about log houses (that they were easy to erect and short-lived) in "Architectural Styles in Preservation," in Kitchen, ed., *The Past Projected: A Perspective on Historic Preservation* (Tiffin, Ohio: Ohio Humanities Council, 1977), p. 4.

10. Collected by Henry C. Belden in his reknowned *Ballads and Songs Collected by the Missouri Folk-Lore Society*, p. 426; a similar variant on the theme is "Arkansas Boys" in Earl A. Collins, *Legends and Lore of Missouri*, pp. 94–95, and the comparative verse is "Some is prepared/With hewed log wall,/With no windows/In them at all,/Sand rock chimney/And a batten door,/Clapboard roof/And a puncheon floor." (The Collins variant is the one popularized in the 1960s by a revival string band, The New Lost City Ramblers.)

11. From my visit with Mr. and Mrs. Griffin in March 1974, when Mr. Griffin was eighty-five; he was the featured "Citizen of the Week" in the *Boone County Top-Journal* on 14 February 1974. Griffin and Mr. Louis Wienhaus from near Mt. Airy in Randolph County gave fine explanations of log-construction methods from personal experience. Mr. Wienhaus demonstrated his hewing technique for me, using a felling ax and broadax; he recently hewed several new sills for his barn. See also Norbert F. Riedl, Donald B. Ball, and Anthony P. Cavender, "Interview with Mr. Onie L. Norton," in *A Survey of Traditional Architecture and Related Folk Culture Patterns in the Normandy Reservoir, Coffee County, Tennessee*, pp. 168–74.

12. For example, there are new books with just enough authenticity to entice the nonspecialist, like Alex W. Bealer and John O. Ellis, *The Log Cabin: Homes of the North American Wilderness* (Barre, Mass.: Barre Publishing Co., 1978), with statements like "The log cabin provided excellent shelter from the driving winds of winter and the drenching rains of spring, and at times the arrows or bullets of savage enemies" (p. 9), "Any man with a modicum of skill with an ax could build his own cabin in a relatively short time if he did not mind hard work" (pp. 9–10), and a restatement of the long-disproved notion that the Swedes spread log construction over pioneer America (p. 11); and there are errors that would not be possible if the writers had done extensive field research, such as the assertion that square-notching is the "easiest" cornering method, found in crude temporary houses (p. 41); and the book contains several passages like "Sometimes, when no chore pressed too hard, men or women would play the fiddle or pluck the gentle dulcimer or pick a guitar or banjo for the sheer joy of controlling the melody or harmony of a tune or ballad" (p. 64); the book lists an impressive bibliography that includes Glassie, Hutslar, Rempel, and Weslager. See also Roger M. Williams,

"The Return of the Log House," with such nonsense as "The pioneers . . . [thought log houses to be temporary] to be abandoned the minute the settlers could manage to build themselves more comfortable frame houses as much as possible like the ones they had left behind back East" (p. 48). Essential references for legitimate access to log construction include Fred Kniffen, "On Corner-Timbering," *Pioneer America* 1:1 (January 1969): 1–18, and Kniffen and Glassie, "Building in Wood"; Charles A. Weslager's *The Log Cabin in America* is the basic broad treatment, and, though dated, Harold R. Shurtleff's *The Log Cabin Myth: A Study of the Early Dwellings of the English Colonists in North America* is still required reading. Warren E. Roberts, "Folk Architecture," in Richard M. Dorson, ed., *Folklore and Folklife: An Introduction*, pp. 281–93; Warren E. Roberts, "Some Comments on Log Construction in Scandinavia and in the United States"; and Warren E. Roberts, "The Tools Used in Building Log Houses in Indiana," *Pioneer America* 9:1 (July 1977): 30–61. Don Hutslar's *The Log Architecture of Ohio* is a model statewide study by an art historian; geographer Terry G. Jordan has written a valuable book on Texas, *Texas Log Buildings: A Folk Architecture*; and see Riedl, Ball, and Cavender, *Survey of Traditional Architecture*, and Wilbur Zelinsky's "The Log House in Georgia."

13. For example, F. D. Srygley, *Seventy Years in Dixie* (Nashville: Gospel Advocate Publishing Co., 1891), pp. 131–38; J. L. Herring, *Saturday Night Sketches* (1918. Reprint, Tifton, Ga.: Sunny South Press, 1978), pp. 268–72; passages in Mark Twain's *Huckleberry Finn* (Scranton, Pa.: Chandler Facsimile Edition, 1962); and Charles P. Mayo, "Allen Mayo," in Howard Wight Marshall, *Old Families of Randolph County, Missouri: A People's History*, pp. 206–20.

14. See Henry Glassie, *Folk Housing in Middle Virginia: A Structural Analysis of Historic Artifacts*, pp. 156–60; the Victorian habit of unrelenting white paint still prevails over much of the Little Dixie landscape.

15. As I put it in "The Thousand Acres Log House, Monroe County, Indiana," p. 56; there is a good discussion of dating problems (and a call for dendrochronology in the United States) in Riedl, Ball, and Cavender, *A Survey of Traditional Architecture*; Glassie, *Folk Housing in Middle Virginia*; and Henry Chapman Mercer's classic *The Dating of Old Houses* (Doylestown, Pa.: Bucks County Historical Society, 1923). In Europe, problems of dating take on proportions that would startle Americans studying, say, log houses in southern Idaho; for example, Karl-Olov Arntsberg has been recording Swedish log buildings dating not to the nineteenth or late seventeenth, but to the twelfth century. See *Datering av knuttimrade hus i Sverige.*

16. See Charles van Ravenswaay, *The Arts and Architecture of German Settlements in Missouri: A Survey of a Vanishing Culture*, pp. 108, 113, 116.

Notes to Chapter 6

1. Interview with Mr. Brown Robinson, aged eighty-four, Rocheport, Boone County, March 1974.

2. Mr. Jennings Franklin Leach, aged sixty-six, near St. Martins, Cole County, and Mr. Ben Cook, aged eighty-five, Tenmile community, Macon County, both in 1974.

3. From recorded interviews in 1974 with Mrs. Ralph Gregory, aged fifty-three, Stoutsville; Mr. Carl T. Bounds, aged seventy, Paris; Mr. Lee Miller, aged sixty-one (1971 interview), Paris; Mr. R. I. "Si" Colburn, aged seventy-five, Paris; Mrs. Charles M. Bush, aged seventy-four, Northfork community; Mr. Charles M. Bush, aged eighty-four, Northfork; Mr. Guy Patton, aged seventy, near Milton; Mrs. Jess Wedding, aged seventy-four, near Levick's Mill; Mr. William Howard Turner, aged sixty-two, near Clifton Hill; Mr. James Augustine Wight, aged seventy-five, Moberly; Mrs. Raymond Dawson, aged sixty-nine, Guthrie community; and Mr. John Wells, aged ninety-two, Fulton.

4. Ronald W. Brunskill, "English Vernacular Architecture," *Journal of the Folklore Institute* 2:3 (December 1965): 300.

Bibliography

Adams, Henry. *The United States in 1800*. 1889. Reprint, Ithaca: Cornell University Press, 1955.

Addy, Sidney Oldall. *Evolution of English House*. London: G. Allen and Unwin, 1933.

Alcott, John V. *Colonial Homes in North Carolina*. Raleigh, N.C.: Division of Archaeology and History, North Carolina Department of Cultural Resources, 1975.

Alexander, Christopher. *Notes on the Synthesis of Form*. Cambridge: Harvard University Press, 1964.

Allen, Harold B., and Underwood, Gary, eds. *Readings in American Dialectology*. New York: Appleton Century Crofts, 1971.

Allen, James L. *The Blue-Grass Region of Kentucky, and Other Kentucky Articles*. New York: Macmillan, 1900.

Arensburg, Conrad M. "American Communities." *American Anthropologist* 57 (1955): 143–62.

———. *The Irish Countryman: An Anthropological Study*. Garden City, N.Y.: Natural History Press, 1968.

Arensburg, Conrad M., and Kimball, Solon T. *Culture and Community*. New York: Harcourt, Brace and World, 1965.

Arnold, B. W., Jr. *History of the Tobacco Industry in Virginia from 1860 to 1894*. Baltimore: Johns Hopkins University Press, 1897.

Arnow, Harriette Simpson. *Seedtime on the Cumberland*. New York: Macmillan Co., 1960.

Arntsberg, Karl-Olov. *Datering av knuttimrade hus i Sverige*. Stockholm: Nordiska Museet, 1976.

Atwood, E. Bagby. *The Regional Vocabulary of Texas*. Austin: University of Texas Press, 1962.

Bagby, George W. *The Old Virginia Gentleman and Other Sketches*. Richmond: Dietz, 1943.

Baggs, A. P. "Pattern Books and Vernacular Architecture before 1790." *Vernacular Architecture* 3 (1972): 22–23.

Balthus, Laura V., ed. *Early Recollections of George W. Dameron and Biographical Sketches of Prominent Citizens of Pioneer Days*. Huntsville, Mo.: Herald Print, 1898.

Barley, Michael W. *The English Farmhouse and Cottage*. London: Routledge and Kegan Paul, 1961.

———. *The House and Home: A Review of 900 Years of House Planning and Furnishing in Great Britain*. Essex: Anchor Press, 1963.

Barnes, H. W., ed. *Recent Developments in the Social Sciences*. New York, 1925.

Barnett, H. G. *Innovation: The Basis of Cultural Change*. New York: McGraw-Hill, 1953.

Barns, Chancy R., ed. *The Commonwealth of Missouri: A Centennial Record*. St. Louis: Bryan, Brand and Co., 1877.

Bateman, James A. *Animal Traps and Trapping*. Newton Abbot, Eng.: David and Charles, 1971.

Batsford, Harry, and Fry, Charles. *The English Cottage*. London: Batsford, 1950.

Beck, Louis Caleb. *A Gazeteer of the States of Illinois and Missouri; containing a General View of Each State, a General View of their Counties, and a Particular Description of their Villages, Rivers, etc., etc.* St. Louis: C. Keemle, 1837.

Beckman, D. F., Jr. "Bull Strong, Pig Tight, Horse High." *New York Times*, 29 April 1973, p. 25.

Beecham, H. A., and Higgs, John. *The Story of Farm Tools*. London: Evans Brothers, 1961.

Bek, William G., trans. "Gottfried Duden's 'Report' 1824–1827." *Missouri Historical Re-*

view 12 (October 1917): 1–21; (January 1918): 81–89; (April 1918): 163–79; (July 1918): 258–70; 13 (October 1918): 44–56; (January 1919): 157–81; (April 1919): 251–81.

Belden, Henry M. *Ballads and Songs Collected by the Missouri Folk-Lore Society*. Columbia: University of Missouri Press, 1955.

Benedict, Ruth. *Patterns of Culture*. New York: Houghton Mifflin Co., 1934.

Beverly, Robert. *The History and Present State of Virginia*. Chapel Hill: University of North Carolina Press, 1947.

Blair, Don. *Harmonist Construction*. Indianapolis: Indiana Historical Society Publications 23:2 (1964).

Boas, Franz. *Primitive Art*. 1927. Reprint, New York: Dover, 1955.

Bogue, Alan G. *From Prairie to Cornbelt: Farming on the Illinois and Iowa Prairies in the Nineteenth Century*. Chicago: University of Chicago Press, 1963.

"Boon's Lick Folk Tales." *Missouri Historical Society Bulletin* 6 (1949–1950): 472–90.

Boorstin, Daniel J. *The Americans: The National Experience*. New York: Random House, 1965.

Bowers, L. *Plantation Recipes*. New York: Robert Speller, 1959.

Brackenridge, Henry Marie. *Recollections of Persons and Places in the West*. 2d ed. Philadelphia: Lippencott and Co., 1868.

———. *Views of Louisiana; together with a Journal of a Voyage up the Missouri River, in 1811*. Pittsburgh: Cramer Spear and Eichbaum, 1814.

Bradley, Chester A. "Little Dixie Is in an Uproar Again about Democracy and Country Ham." *Kansas City Times*, 31 May 1948.

Briggs, Martin S. *The English Farmhouse*. London: Batsford, 1953.

———. *Homes of the Pilgrim Fathers in England and America, 1620–1685*. New York: Oxford University Press, 1932.

Brigham, Albert P. *Geographic Influences in American History*. Boston: Ginn, 1925.

Brown, Ralph H. *Historical Geography of the United States*. New York: Harcourt, Brace and World, 1948.

Browne, Walter A. *Missouri Geography*. Oklahoma City: Harlow Publishing Corporation, 1956.

Brownell, Joseph W. "The Cultural Midwest." *Journal of Geography* 39 (February 1960): 81–85.

Brownlee, Richard S. *Grey Ghosts of the Confederacy: Guerilla Warfare in the West, 1861–1865*. Baton Rouge: Louisiana State University Press, 1958.

Brunskill, Ronald W. *Illustrated Handbook of Vernacular Architecture*. London: Faber and Faber, 1970.

———. "A Systematic Procedure for Recording English Vernacular Architecture." *Transactions of the Ancient Monument Society* 13 (1965–1966): 42–126.

———. *Vernacular Architecture of the Lake Counties*. London: Faber and Faber, 1974.

Brunvand, Jan H. *The Study of American Folklore*. New York: W. W. Norton, 1968.

Bryan, John A. *Missouri's Contribution to American Architecture*. St. Louis: St. Louis Architectural Club, 1928.

Bryan, W. S. *A History of Pioneer Families of Missouri*. St. Louis: Bryan, Brand and Co., 1876.

Buchanan, Ronald H. "A Decade of Folklife Study." *Ulster Folklife* 11 (1965): 63–75.

———. "Geography and Folk Life." *Folk Life* 1 (1963): 1–15.

Buchanan, Ronald H.; McCourt, D.; and Jones, E. *Man and His Habitat: Essays in Honor of Emyr Estyn Evans*. London: Routledge and Kegan Paul, 1971.

Bucher, Robert C. "The Continental Log House." *Pennsylvania Folklife* 12:4 (Summer 1962): 14–19.

———. "The First Shelters of Our Pilgrim Ancestors." *Pioneer America* 1:2 (July 1969): 7–12.

Buie, T. S. "Rail Fences." *American Forests* 70:10 (October 1964): 44–46.

Burns, C. R., ed. *Switzler's Illustrated History of Missouri from 1541 to 1877*. St. Louis: C. R. Burns, 1879.

Campbell, John C. *The Southern Highlander and His Homeland*. New York: Russell Sage, 1921.

Capon, Lester J., ed. *Atlas of Early American History*. Princeton: Princeton University Press, 1976.

Carr, Lucien. *Missouri a Bone of Contention*. Boston: Houghton Mifflin, 1888.

Carrière, Joseph M. *Tales from the French Folk-Lore of Missouri*. Evanston, Ill., Northwestern University Studies, 1937.

Carson, Cary. "The 'Virginia House' in Maryland." *Maryland Historical Magazine* 69:2 (Summer 1974): 185–96.

Carter, Thomas. "The Joel Cock House: Meadows of Dan, Patrick County, Virginia." *Southern Folklore Quarterly* 39:4 (December 1975): 329–40.

Cassidy, Frederic G. "The Meaning of 'Regional' in *DARE*." *American Speech* 48:3–4 (Fall–Winter 1973): 282–89.

Chapman, Carl H., and Chapman, Eleanor F. *Indians and Archaeology of Missouri*. Missouri Handbook No. 6. Columbia: University of Missouri Press, 1966.

Chisolm, Michael. *Rural Settlement and Land Use: An Essay in Location*. New York: John Wiley and Sons, 1967.

Clark, B. H. *The Tennessee Yeoman, 1840–1860*. Nashville: Vanderbilt University Press, 1942.

Clark, Dan Elbert. *The Middle West in American History*. New York: Thomas Y. Crowell, 1937.

Clark, Thomas D. *Frontier America*. New York: Scribners, 1959.

———. *The Kentucky*. New York: Farrar and Rinehart, 1942.

Clifton-Taylor, Alec. *The Pattern in English Building*. London: Faber and Faber, 1972.

Collins, Earl A. *Legends and Lore of Missouri*. San Antonio: The Naylor Co., 1951.

Collins, Earl A., and Elsea, Albert F. *Missouri: Its People and Its Progress*. St. Louis and Dallas: Webster Publishing Co., 1945.

Collins, Earl A., and Snider, Felix E. *Missouri: A History of the Midland State*. St. Louis and Dallas: Webster Publishing Co., 1955.

Commager, Henry Steele. *The American Mind: An Interpretation of American Thought and Character Since the 1880's*. New Haven: Yale University Press, 1950.

———. *The Blue and the Gray: The Story of the Civil War as Told by Participants*. Indianapolis: Bobbs-Merrill, 1950.

Condit, Carl. *American Building*. Chicago: University of Chicago Press, 1968.

Confederate Home Association of Missouri. *Missouri of To-Day. Progress and Prospects of the Great Commercial State and Center of Population Its Chief Cities and Towns including Reminiscences of "Missouri in 1861."* Higginsville, Mo.: Confederate Home Association of Missouri, 1893.

Conroy, Jack. *The Disinherited*. New York: Hill and Wang, 1933.

Couch, William T. *Culture in the South*. Chapel Hill: University of North Carolina Press, 1934.

Coulter, Willis M. *The Confederate States of America, 1861–1865*. Baton Rouge: Louisiana State University Press, 1950.

———. *The South during Reconstruction, 1865–77*. Baton Rouge: Louisiana State University Press, 1947.

Croy, Homer. *Corn Country*. New York: Duell, Sloan and Pearce, American Folkways Series, 1947.

———. *Country Cured*. New York: Harper's, 1943.

Cummings, Abbott Lowell. *Architecture in Early New England*. Sturbridge, Mass.: Old Sturbridge Village, 1974.

———. *The Framed Houses of Massachusetts Bay, 1625–1725*. Cambridge, Mass.: Harvard University Press, 1979.

Deetz, James. *In Small Things Forgotten: The Architecture of Early American Life*. Garden City, N.Y.: Anchor Press, 1977.

Deetz, James, ed. *Man's Imprint from the Past: Readings in the Methods of Archaeology*. Boston: Little, Brown, 1971.

DePillis, Mario. "Folklore and the American West." *Arizona and the West* 4:4 (1963): 291–314.

Dick, Everett. *The Dixie Frontier*. New York: Capricorn Books, 1964.

Dohrs, Fred E., and Sommers, Lawrence M., eds. *Cultural Geography: Selected Readings*. New York: Thomas Y. Crowell, 1967.

Dorrance, Ward A. *The Survival of French in the Old District of Sainte Genevieve*. Columbia, Mo., 1935.

Dorson, Richard M. *American Folklore*. Chicago: University of Chicago Press, 1959.

———. *Buying the Wind: Regional Folklore in the United States*. Chicago: University of Chicago Press, 1964.

———. "Discussion from the Floor" on Dorson, "A Theory for American Folklore." *Journal of American Folklore* 72:285 (1959): 238.

Dorson, Richard M., ed. *Folklore and Folklife: An Introduction*. Chicago: University of Chicago Press, 1972.

Downing, Andrew Jackson. *The Architecture of Country Houses*. 1850. Reprint, New York: Dover Publications, 1969.

Downs, Lawrence A. *The Greatness of the Middle West*. Sioux City, Iowa: Illinois Central System, 1928.

Drake, D., and Horrine, E. F., eds. *Pioneer Life in Kentucky, 1785–1800*. New York: Henry Schuman, 1948.

Dundes, Alan. "From Etic to Emic Units in the Structural Study of Folktales." *Journal of American Folklore* 75:296 (1962): 95–105.

———. "Texture, Text, and Context." *Southern Folklore Quarterly* 28:4 (1964): 251–65.

Dundes, Alan, ed. *The Study of Folklore*. Englewood Cliffs, N.J.: Prentice-Hall, 1965.

Eaton, Allen H. *Handicrafts of the Southern Highlands*. New York: Russell Sage Foundation, 1937.

Eaton, Clement. *A History of the Southern Confederacy*. New York: Macmillan, 1954.

Eaton, David W. *How Missouri Counties, Towns, and Streams Were Named*. Columbia: State Historical Society of Missouri, 1916.

Ellis, James Fernando. *The Influence of Environment on the Settlement of Missouri*. St. Louis: Webster Publishing Co., 1929.

Emerson, E. V. *Geography of Missouri*. Columbia: University of Missouri Bulletin, Educational Series 1:4 (1912).

Erixon, Sigurd. "Folklife Research in Our Time." *Gwerin* 3 (1962): 271–91.

———. "An Introduction to Folklife Research or Nordic Ethnology." *Folk-Liv* 14 (1950): 5–15.

———. "The North-European Technique of Corner Timbering." *Folk-Liv* 1 (1937): 13–60.

———. "Regional European Ethnology." *Folk-Liv* 1 (1937): 2–3, 89–108; 2 (1938): 3, 263–94.

Esarey, Logan. *The Indiana Home*. Bloomington: Indiana University Press, 1953.

Evans, E. Estyn. "Cultural Relics of the Ulster Scots in the Old West of North America." *Ulster Folklife* 11 (1965): 33–38.

———. "Folklife Studies in Northern Ireland." *Journal of the Folklore Institute* 2:3 (December 1965): 355–63.

———. *Irish Folk Ways*. London: Routledge and Kegan Paul, 1957.

———. *Mourne Country: Landscape and Life in South Down*. Dundalk, N. Ire.: Dundalgan Press, 1967.

———. "The Ulster Farmhouse." *Ulster Folklife* 1 (1955): 17–31.

Evans, George Ewart. *Ask the Fellows Who Cut the Hay*. London: Faber and Faber, 1956.

———. *Tools of Their Trade: An Oral History of Men at Work c. 1900*. New York: Taplinger Publishing Co., 1970.

Faries, Rachel B. "A Survey of the Vocabulary of Seven North East Central Missouri Counties." Master's thesis, University of Missouri, 1954.

———. "A Word Geography of Missouri." Ph.D. thesis, University of Missouri, 1967.

"The Farm Housing Survey." United States Department of Agriculture Miscellaneous Publication No. 323 (1939).

Faust, Albert B. *The German Influence in the United States with Special Reference to Its Political, Moral, Social, and Educational Influence*. 2 vols. Boston: Houghton, 1909.

Federal Writers' Project, Works Progress Administration. *Kentucky: A Guide to the Bluegrass State*. New York: Harcourt, Brace, 1942.

———. *Missouri: A Guide to the "Show-Me" State*. New York: Duell, Sloan and Pearce, 1941.

Fenton, Alexander. "An Approach to Folk Life Studies." *Keystone Folklore Quarterly* 12:1 (1967): 5–21.

———. "Material Culture as an Aid to Local History Studies in Scotland." *Journal of the Folklore Institute* 2:3 (December 1965): 326–39.

———. "The Scope of Regional Ethnology." *Folk Life* 11 (1973): 5–14.

Ferguson, Leland, ed. *Historical Archaeology and the Importance of Material Things*. Washington, D.C.: Society for Historical Archaeology, Publications Series No. 2, 1977.

Fife, Austin; Fife, Alta; and Glassie, Henry, eds. *Forms upon the Frontier*. Logan: Utah State University Press, 1969.

Fitch, James Marston. *American Building: The Forces that Shape It*. Boston: Houghton Mifflin Co., 1948.

Fletcher, Stevenson W. *Pennsylvania Agriculture and Country Life, 1640–1840*. Harrisburg: Pennsylvania Historical & Museum Commission, 1950.

Fontana, Bernard L. "Bottles, Buckets and Horseshoes: The Unrespectable in American Archaeology." *Keystone Folklore Quarterly* 13:3 (1968): 171–84.

Forman, Henry C. *The Architecture of the Old South: The Medieval Style, 1585–1850*. Cambridge, Mass.: Harvard University Press, 1948.

———. *Old Buildings, Gardens and Furniture of Tidewater Maryland*. Easton: Tidewater Publishers, 1967.

———. *Tidewater Maryland Architecture and Gardens*. New York: Bonanza Books, 1956.

Foster, George M. "What Is Folk Culture?" *American Anthropologist* 55:2, 1 (April–June 1953): 159–73.

Foster, I. L., and Alcock, L., eds. *Culture and Environment: Essays in Honor of Sir Cyril Fox*. London: Routledge and Kegan Paul, 1963.

Fox, Sir Cyril. *The Personality of Britain: Its Influence on Inhabitant and Invader in Prehistoric and Early Historic Times*. Cardiff: National Museum of Wales, 1932.

Fox, Sir Cyril, and Raglan, Lord. *Monmouthshire Houses: A Study of Building Techniques and Smaller House-Plans in the Fifteenth to Seventeenth Centuries*. 3 vols. Cardiff: National Museum of Wales, 1951–1954.

Fussell, George E. *The Farmer's Tools, A.D. 1500–1900*. London: Andrew Melrose, 1952.

Gailey, Alan. "The Peasant Houses of the South-west Highlands of Scotland: Distribution, Parallels and Evolution." *Gwerin* 3 (1960–1962): 227–42.

Garland, John H., ed. *The North American Midwest: A Regional Geography*. New York: John Wiley, 1955.

Garner, Wightman W. *The Production of Tobacco*. Rev. ed. New York: The Blakiston Co., 1951.

Garret, Mitchell B. *Horse and Buggy Days on Hatchet Creek*. University, Ala.: University of Alabama Press, 1964.

Gates, Paul W. *The Farmer's Age: Agriculture, 1815–1860*. New York: Holt, Rinehart, and Winston, 1960.

———. "Southern Investments in Northern Lands before the Civil War." *Journal of South-*

ern History 5 (May 1939): 155–85.

Gillin, John. "National and Regional Cultural Values in the United States." *Social Forces* 34 (December 1955): 107–13.

Glassie, Henry Haywood, III. "The Appalachian Log Cabin." *Mountain Life and Work* 39:4 (Winter 1963): 5–14.

———. "Barns across Southern England: A Note on Transatlantic Comparisons and Architectural Meanings." *Pioneer America* 7:1 (1975): 9–19.

———. "A Central Chimney Continental Log House." *Pennsylvania Folklife* 18:2 (Winter 1968–1969): 32–39.

———. "The Double-Crib Barn in South Central Pennsylvania." *Pioneer America* 1:1 (January 1969): 9–16; 1:2 (July 1969): 40–45; 2:1 (January 1970): 47–52; 2:2 (July 1970): 23–34.

———. *Folk Housing in Middle Virginia: A Structural Analysis of Historic Artifacts.* Knoxville: University of Tennessee Press, 1975.

———. "The Impact of the Georgian Form on American Folk Housing" (abstract). In Austin Fife, Alta Fife, and Henry Glassie, eds., *Forms upon the Frontier*, pp. 23–25. Logan: Utah State University Press, 1969.

———. "The Old Barns of Appalachia." *Mountain Life and Work* 40:2 (Summer 1965): 21–30.

———. *Pattern in the Material Folk Culture of the Eastern United States.* Philadelphia: University of Pennsylvania Press, 1968.

———. "The Pennsylvania Barn in the South." *Pennsylvania Folklife* 15:2 (Winter 1965–1966): 8–19; 15:4 (Summer 1966): 12–25.

———. "The Smaller Outbuildings of the Southern Mountains." *Mountain Life and Work* 40:1 (Spring 1964): 21–25.

———. "The Types of the Southern Mountain Cabin." In Jan H. Brunvand, *The Study of American Folklore*, pp. 338–70. New York: W. W. Norton, 1968.

———. "The Variation of Concepts within Tradition: Barn Building in Otsego County, New York." In H. J. Walker and W. G. Haag, eds., *Man and Cultural Heritage: Papers in Honor of Fred B. Kniffen*, pp. 177–235. Baton Rouge: Louisiana State University School of Geoscience, 1974.

———. "The Wedderspoon Farm." *New York Folklore Quarterly* 22:3 (September 1966): 165–87.

Goodenough, Ward H. *Cooperation in Change.* New York: Russell Sage Foundation, 1963.

Goodwin, Cardinal. *The Trans-Mississippi West, 1803–1853: A History of Its Acquisition and Settlement.* New York: Appleton, Century, Crofts, 1922.

Gordon, John B. *Reminiscences of the Civil War.* New York: Scribners, 1903.

Gott, Theresa, and Vlach, John Michael. "The Bucklodge House: Eighteenth and Nineteenth Century Traditions on a Montgomery County Farm." *Free State Folklore* 4:1 (Winter 1977): 35–58.

Gould, Mary Earle. *The Early American House: Household Life in America, 1620–1850.* Rutland, Vt.: C. E. Tuttle, 1965.

Gowans, Alan. *Images of American Living: Four Centuries of Architecture and Furniture as Cultural Expression.* New York: Harper and Row, 1964.

Grant, Isabel. *Highland Folk Ways.* London: Routledge and Kegan Paul, 1961.

Gray, Lewis Cecil. *History of Agriculture in the Southern United States to 1860.* 2 vols. Washington, D.C.: Carnegie Institute, 1933.

Greene, Donald P. "Prairie Agricultural Technology, 1860–1900." Ph.D. dissertation, Indiana University, 1957.

Gunther, John. *Inside USA.* New York: Harper Brothers, 1947.

Hall, J. S. *Smoky Mountain Folks and Their Lore.* Asheville, S.C.: Great Smoky Mountains Natural History Association, 1964.

Hall, Robert B. "The Geographic Region: A Resumé." *Annals of the Association of Ameri-*

    can Geographers 25 (1935): 121–74.

Hall, Robert de Zouche, ed. *A Bibliography of Vernacular Architecture*. Newton Abbot, Eng.: David and Charles for the Vernacular Architecture Group, 1972.

Hamilton, James A. "The Enrolled Missouri Militia: Its Creation and Controversial History." *Missouri Historical Review* 69:4 (1975): 413–33.

Hamilton, Jean Tyree, comp. *Arrow Rock: Where Wheels Started West*. Centralia, Mo.: Guard Printing and Publishing Co., 1963.

Hammar, C. F.; Roth, W. J.; and Johnson, O. R. *Types of Farming in Missouri*. Columbia: University of Missouri College of Agriculture Experiment Station Research Bulletin 284, 1938.

Harney, G. E. *Barns, Outbuildings and Fences*. New York: George E. Woodward, 1970.

———. "The Character of Tobacco Barns and Their Role in the Tobacco Economy of the United States." *Annals of the Association of American Geographers* 51:3 (1961): 274–93.

Harris, Marvin. *The Nature of Cultural Things*. New York: Random House, 1964.

———. *The Rise of Anthropological Theory*. New York: Thomas Y. Crowell, 1968.

Hart, Albert B. *Slavery and Abolition, 1831–1841*. New York: Harper, 1906.

Hart, John Fraser. *The Look of the Land*. Englewood Cliffs, N.J.: Prentice-Hall, 1975.

———. *The Southeastern United States*. New York: Van Nostrand Reinhold Co., 1967.

Hart, John Fraser, and Mather, Eugene Cotton. "The American Fence." *Landscape* 6:3 (1957): 4–9.

Haystead, Ladd, and Fite, Gilbert C. *Agricultural Regions of the United States*. Norman: University of Oklahoma Press, 1955.

Henderson, Archibald. *The Conquest of the Old Southwest: The Romantic Story of the Early Pioneers into Virginia, the Carolinas, Tennessee, and Kentucky, 1740–1790*. New York: Century, 1920.

Henry, Robert S. *The Story of Reconstruction*. Indianapolis: Bobbs-Merrill, 1938.

Herman, Bernard L., and Orr, David G. "Pear Valley et al.: An Excursion into the Analysis of Southern Vernacular Architecture." *Southern Folklore Quarterly* 39:4 (December 1975): 307–28.

Herskovits, Melville J. *Acculturation: The Study of Culture Contact*. New York: J. J. Augustin, 1938.

Higgs, J. W. Y. *Folk Life Collection and Classification*. London: Museum Association, 1963.

Higham, John. *Strangers in the Land: Patterns of American Nativism, 1860–1925*. New Brunswick, N.J.: Rutgers University Press, 1955.

History of Callaway County, Missouri. . . . St. Louis: National Historical Company, 1884.

History of Macon and Randolph Counties, Missouri. . . . St. Louis: National Historical Company, 1884.

History of Monroe and Shelby Counties, Missouri. . . . St. Louis: National Historical Company, 1884.

Horsbrugh, P. "Barns in Central Illinois." *Landscape* 8:3 (Spring 1950): 12–13.

Hoskins, Jewell M. "A Survey of the Vocabulary of Seven Eastern Missouri Valley Counties." Master's thesis, University of Missouri, 1954.

Hoskins, W. G. *Fieldwork in Local History*. London: Faber and Faber, 1967.

———. "The Rebuilding of Rural England, 1570–1640." *Past and Present* 4 (1953): 44–57.

Houck, Louis. *History of Missouri*. 3 vols. Chicago: R. R. Donnelly, 1908.

Howard, Perry H. *Political Tendencies in Louisiana, 1812–1952*. Baton Rouge: Louisiana State University Studies, No. 5, 1960.

Hulbert, Archer Butler. *Soil: Its Influence on American History with Special Reference to Migration and Scientific Study of Local History*. New Haven: Yale University Press, 1930.

Hutslar, Donald. *The Log Architecture of Ohio*. Columbus: Ohio Historical Society, 1971.

Hyatt, Henry Middleton. *Folk-Lore from Adams County, Illinois*. New York: Memoirs of the Alma Egan Hyatt Foundation, 1935.

Innocent, C. F. *The Development of English Building Construction*. 1916. Reprint, London: David and Charles, 1971.

Jackson, J. B. *On the Necessity for Ruins, and Other Topics*. Amherst: University of Massachusetts Press, 1980.

Jenkins, J. Geraint. "Field-Work and Documentation in Folk-Life Studies." *Journal of the Royal Anthropological Institute* 90 (1960): 259–71.

Jenkins, J. Geraint, ed. *Studies in Folklife: Essays in Honor of Iorwerth C. Peate*. New York: Barnes and Noble, 1969.

Jenkins, J. Geraint, and Jewell, C. A. *Recording Rural Life*. Reading: Museum of English Rural Life Report, 1957.

Jensen, Merrill, ed. *Regionalism in America*. Madison: University of Wisconsin Press, 1951.

Johnson, Alan H. "Rocheport, Missouri: A Study in Economic Geography." Master's thesis, University of Missouri, 1962.

Johnson, C. "Missouri-French Houses: Some Relict Features of Early Settlement." *Pioneer America* 6:2 (1947): 1–11.

Johnston, Frances Benjamin, and Waterman, Thomas Tileston. *The Early Architecture of North Carolina*. Chapel Hill: University of North Carolina Press, 1947.

Jones, Emrys. *Human Geography*. London: Chatto and Windus, 1964.

Jones, Wellington D. "Procedures in Investigation of Human Occupance of a Region." *Annals of the Association of American Geographers* 24 (1934): 93–107.

Jones, William L. "Hugo of Rocheport." *Western Folklore* 20 (1961): 23–25.

Jordan, J. G. "Between the Forest and Prairie." *Agricultural History* 38 (1964): 205–16.

Jordan, Terry G. "The Imprint of the Upper and Lower South on Mid-Nineteenth Century Texas." *Annals of the Association of American Geographers* 57:4 (1967): 667–90.

———. "The Texas Appalachia." *Annals of the Association of American Geographers* 60 (1970): 409–27.

———. *Texas Log Buildings: A Folk Architecture*. Austin: University of Texas Press, 1978.

Kantor, MacKinlay. *Missouri Bittersweet*. Garden City, N.Y.: Doubleday, 1969.

———. *The Voice of Bugle Ann*. New York: Coward-McCann, 1935.

Kaufman, Henry J. "Literature on Log Architecture: A Survey." *The Pennsylvania Dutchman* 7 (1955): 30–34.

Kelly, J. F. *The Early Domestic Architecture of Connecticut*. New Haven: Yale University Press, 1924.

Kephart, Horace. *Our Southern Highlanders*. New York: Macmillan Co., 1921.

Key, V. O., Jr. *Southern Politics*. New York: Alfred A. Knopf, 1949.

Key, Vladimir, and Heard, Alexander. *Southern Politics in State and Nation*. New York: Alfred A. Knopf, 1949.

Kimball, Fisek. *Domestic Architecture of the American Colonies and of the Early Republic*. 1922. Reprint, New York: Dover, 1966.

Kirkpatrick, Arthur R. "Missouri, the Twelfth Confederate State." Master's thesis, University of Missouri, 1954.

Kniffen, Fred B. "Folk Housing: Key to Diffusion." *Annals of the Association of American Geographers* 55 (1965): 549–77.

———. "Louisiana House Types." *Annals of the Association of American Geographers* 26 (1936): 179–93.

———. "To Know the Land and Its People." *Landscape* 9:3 (Spring 1960): 20–23.

Kniffen, Fred B., and Glassie, Henry. "Building in Wood in the Eastern United States: A Time-Place Perspective." *The Geographical Review* 56 (1966): 40–66.

Kniffen, Fred B., and Russell, R. J. *Culture Worlds*. New York: Macmillan Co., 1951.

Koontz, Louis K. *The Virginia Frontier, 1754–1763*. Baltimore: Johns Hopkins University Press, 1925.

Kouwenhoven, John A. *The Arts in American Civilization*. New York: W. W. Norton, 1967.

Kramer, Frank R. *Voices in the Valley: Mythmaking and Folk Belief in the Shaping of the Middle West*. Madison: University of Wisconsin Press, 1964.

Kroeber, Alfred. *Cultural and Natural Areas of Native North America*. Berkeley: University of California Publications in American Archaeology and Ethnology, vol. 38, 1939.

Kubler, George. *The Shape of Time: Remarks on the History of Things*. New Haven and London: Yale University Press, 1962.

Kuhn, Thomas S. *The Structure of Scientific Revolutions*. Chicago: University of Chicago Press, 1972.

Kurath, Hans. "Dialect Areas, Settlement Areas, and Cultural Areas in the United States." In C. F. Ware, ed., *The Cultural Approach to History*, pp. 331–51. New York: Columbia University Press, 1940.

———. "Linguistic Regionalism." In Merrill Jensen, ed., *Regionalism in America*, pp. 297–310. Madison: University of Wisconsin Press, 1951.

———. *A Word Geography of the Eastern United States*. Ann Arbor: University of Michigan Press, 1949.

La Flesche, Francis. "The Osage Tribe." In *Annual Report of the Bureau of American Ethnology* 36: 37–604. Washington, D.C.: Bureau of American Ethnology, 1921.

Lancaster, C. *Ante Bellum Houses of the Bluegrass*. Lexington: University Press of Kentucky, 1961.

Larkin, Lew. *Vanguard of Empire: Missouri's Century of Expansion*. St. Louis: State Publishing Co., 1961.

Laslett, Peter. *The World We Have Lost*. New York: Scribners, 1965.

Latrobe, Charles Joseph. *Rambles in North America, 1832–1833*. New York: Harper and Brothers, 1835.

Leach, MacEdward. "Folklore in American Regional Literature." *Journal of the Folklore Institute* 3:3 (December 1966): 376–97.

Leach, MacEdward, and Glassie, Henry H. *A Guide for Collectors of Oral Tradition and Folk Cultural Material in Pennsylvania*. Harrisburg: Pennsylvania Historical and Museum Commission, 1968.

Leechman, D. "Good Fences Make Good Neighbors." *Canadian Geographical Journal* 47:6 (December 1953): 218–35.

Leighly, John, ed. *Land and Life: A Selection from the Writings of Carl Ortwin Sauer*. Berkeley: University of California Press, 1967.

Lemmer, George F. "The Early Agricultural Fairs of Missouri." *Agricultural History* 17 (1943): 145–52.

Lemon, James T. *The Best Poor Man's Country: A Geographical Study of Early Southeastern Pennsylvania*. Baltimore and London: Johns Hopkins University Press, 1972.

———. "Household Consumption in Eighteenth-Century America and Its Relationship to Production and Trade: The Situation among Farmers in Southeastern Pennsylvania." *Agricultural History* 41 (January 1967): 59–70.

Lewis, Pierce F. "Common Houses, Cultural Spoor." *Landscape* 19:2 (January 1975): 1–22.

———. "The Geography of Old Houses." *Earth and Mineral Sciences* 39:5 (February 1970): 33–37.

Linton, Ralph. "The Concept of National Character." In A. H. Stanton and S. E. Perry, eds., *Personality and Political Crisis*, pp. 133–50. New York: Free Press, 1951.

———. *The Cultural Background of Personality*. New York: Appleton-Century Crofts, 1945.

———. "Nativistic Movements." In William Lessa and Evan Vogt, eds., *Reader in Comparative Religion*, pp. 499–505. New York: Harper and Row, 1965.

Loehr, Rodney C. "Self-Sufficiency on the Farm." *Agricultural History* 26 (1952): 37–41.

Ludwig, G. N. "The Influence of the Pennsylvania Dutch in the Middle West." *The Pennsylvania German Folklore Society* 10 (1945): 1–101.

Lynes, Russell. *The Tastemakers*. New York: Grosset and Dunlap, 1949.

McAvoy, Thomas T., et al. *The Midwest: Myth or Reality?* Notre Dame, Ind.: University of Notre Dame Press, 1961.

McDermott, John F., ed. *Frenchmen and French Ways in the Mississippi Valley*. Englewood Cliffs, N.J.: Prentice-Hall, 1966.

McKee, Harley J., comp. *Recording Historic Buildings*. Washington, D.C.: U.S. Department of Interior, 1970.

MacNamara, Emily Steinestel. *History of Missouri in Words of One Syllable*. Chicago, New York, and San Francisco: Belford Clarke & Co., 1889.

Madden, Betty I. *Arts, Crafts, and Architecture in Early Illinois*. Urbana: University of Illinois Press, 1974.

Mangus, A. R. *Rural Regions of the United States*. Washington, D.C.: Works Progress Administration, 1940.

March, David D. *A History of Missouri*. 4 Vols. New York: Lewis Historical Publishing Co., 1966.

Marshall, Howard Wight. *American Folk Architecture: A Selected Bibliography*. Washington, D.C.: Publications of the American Folklife Center, No. 8, 1981.

———. "Dogtrot Comfort: A Note on Traditional Houses and Energy Efficiency." In *Festival of American Folklife 1980*, pp. 29–31. Washington, D.C.: Smithsonian Institution, 1980.

———. "Meat Preservation on the Farm in Missouri's Little Dixie." *Journal of American Folklore* 92–366 (October–December 1979): 400–417.

———. "Mr. Westfall's Baskets: Traditional Craftsmanship in Northcentral Missouri." *Mid-South Folklore* 2:2 (1974): 43–60.

———. "The Thousand Acres Log House, Monroe County, Indiana." *Pioneer America* 4:1 (January 1971): 48–56.

Marshall, Howard Wight, ed. *Old Families of Randolph County, Missouri: A People's History*. Marceline, Mo.: Walsworth Publishing Co., 1976.

Marshall, Howard Wight, and Vlach, John Michael. "Toward a Folklife Approach to American Dialects." *American Speech* 48:3–4 (Fall–Winter 1973): 163–91.

Marshall, Howard Wight, and Jabbour, Alan. "Folklife and Cultural Preservation." In Robert E. Stipe, ed., *New Directions in Rural Preservation*, pp. 43–50. Washington, D.C.: Heritage Conservation and Recreation Service, U.S. Department of Interior, 1980.

Marzio, Peter C. "Carpentry in the Southern Colonies during the Eighteenth Century with Emphasis on Virginia and Maryland." *Winterthur Portfolio* 7 (1972): 229–50.

Mather, E. C., and Hart, John Fraser. "Fences and Farms." *Geographical Review* 44:2 (1954): 201–23.

Meining, Donald W. *Imperial Texas: An Interpretive Essay in Cultural Geography*. Austin: University of Texas Press, 1969.

———. "The Mormon Culture Region: Strategies and Patterns in the Geography of the American West." *Annals of the Association of American Geographers* 55:2 (1965): 213–17.

Mercer, Eric. *English Vernacular Houses: A Study of Traditional Farmhouses and Cottages*. London: Her Majesty's Stationary Office, 1975.

Mercer, Henry C. *Ancient Carpenters' Tools*. Doylestown, Pa.: Bucks County Historical Society, 1960.

———. "The Origin of Log Houses in the United States." *A Collection of Papers Read Before the Bucks County Historical Society* 5 (1926): 568–83.

Meyer, Duane. *The Heritage of Missouri: A History*. St. Louis: State Publishing Co., 1973.

Miller, Merritt F. *A Century of Missouri Agriculture*. Columbia: University of Missouri Agriculture Experiment Station, Bulletin 701, 1958.

Miner, Horace. *Culture and Agriculture: An Anthropological Study of a Corn Belt County.* Ann Arbor: University of Michigan Press, 1949.

Missouri Democract: A History of the Party and Its Representative Members—Past and Present. 3 vols. Chicago, St. Louis, and Indianapolis: S. J. Clarke Publishing Co., 1935.

Missouri State Park Board. *Foundations from the Past.* Columbia: Missouri State Historical Survey and Planning Office, 1971.

Montell, W. Lynwood. *The Saga of Coe Ridge.* Knoxville: University of Tennessee Press, Harper Torchbooks edition, 1972.

Morland, J. Kenneth. *The Not So Solid South.* Proceedings of the Southern Anthropological Association 4, 1970.

Morrison, Hugh. *Early American Architecture from the First Colonial Settlements to the National Period.* New York: Oxford University Press, 1952.

Mott, Frank Luther, ed. *Missouri Reader.* Columbia: University of Missouri Press, 1964.

Mumford, Lewis. *Roots of Contemporary American Architecture.* New York: Grove Press, 1959.

Murtagh, William J. "Half-Timbering in American Architecture." *Pennsylvania Folklife* 9:1 (1957–1958): 3–11.

Nagel, Paul C. *Missouri: A Bicentennial History.* New York: W.W. Norton, 1977.

Newcomb, Rexford. *Architecture of the Old Northwest Territory.* Chicago: University of Chicago Press, 1950.

———. *Old Kentucky Architecture.* New York: Bonanza Books, 1940.

Nifong, F. G. *The Afterglow.* Columbia, Mo.: Artcraft Press, 1945.

Norberg-Schulz, Christian. *Intentions in Architecture.* Cambridge: M.I.T. Press, 1965.

"Notes and Comments." *Missouri Historical Review* 43:1 (November 1951): 83–84.

Odum, Howard. "Folk Sociology as a Subject Field for the Historical Study of Total Human Society and Empirical Study of Group Behavior." *Social Forces* 31 (1953): 192–223.

———. *Southern Regions of the United States.* Chapel Hill: University of North Carolina Press, 1936.

Odum, Howard W., and Moore, Harry Estill. *American Regionalism: A Cultural-Historical Approach to National Integration.* New York: Holt, Rinehart and Winston, 1938.

Owen, Trefor M. "The Recording of Past Social Conditions." *Folk Life* 4 (1966): 85–89.

Owsley, Frank I. *Plain Folk of the Old South.* Baton Rouge: Louisiana State University Press, 1949.

Pace, Nadine. "Place Names in the Central Counties of Missouri." Master's thesis, University of Missouri, 1928.

Parker, Nathan H. *Missouri As It Is in 1867: An Illustrated Historical Gazateer of Missouri, Embracing the Geography, History, Resources and Prospects; the Mineralogical and Agricultural Wealth and Advantages; the Population, Business Statistics, Public Institutions, etc. of each County in the State.* Philadelphia: J. B. Lippincott and Co., 1867.

Patrick, Rembert W. *The Reconstruction of the Nation.* New York: Oxford University Press, 1967.

Paullin, Charles O. *Atlas of the Historical Geography of the United States.* Edited by John K. Wright. Washington, D.C., and New York: 1932.

Peate, Iorwerth C., *Tradition and Folk Life: A Welsh View.* London: Routledge and Kegan Paul, 1972.

———. *The Welsh House: A Study in Folk Culture.* Liverpool: Hugh Evans, 1944.

Peate, Iorwerth C., ed. *Studies in Regional Consciousness and Environment.* Freeport, N.Y.: Books for Libraries Press, 1968.

Peattie, Roderick, ed. *The Great Smokies and the Blue Ridge: The Story of the Southern Appalachians.* New York: Vanguard Press, 1943.

Pederson, Lee A. "Mark Twain's Missouri Dialects: Marion County Phonemics." *American Speech* 42:4 (December 1967): 261–78.

Perrin, Richard W. E. *Wisconsin Architecture*. Washington, D.C.: Historic American Buildings Survey, U.S. Department of Interior, 1965.

Peterson, C. E. "Early Ste. Genevieve and Its Architecture." *Missouri Historical Review* 35:2 (January 1941): 207–32.

Peterson, William J. "The Pioneer Cabin." *Iowa Journal of History and Politics* 36 (October 1938): 387–409.

Power, Richard Lyle. *Planting Corn Belt Culture: The Impress of the Upland Southerner and Yankee in the Old Northwest*. Indianapolis: Indiana Historical Society, 1953.

Price, E. T. "The American Courthouse Square in the American County Seat." *Geographical Review* 58 (1969): 29–60.

Prince, Hugh C. "Three Realms of Historic Geography: Real, Imagined, and Abstract Worlds of the Past." *Progress in Geography* 3 (1971): 4–86.

Quimby, Ian M. G., ed. *Material Culture and the Study of American Life*. Toronto: George J. McLeod, 1978.

Raithel, Erna E. "A Survey of the Vocabulary of Eight West Central Missouri Counties." Master's thesis, University of Missouri, 1954.

Randolph, Vance. *Ozark Mountain Folks*. New York: Vanguard Press, 1932.

Rapoport, Amos. *House Form and Culture*. Englewood Cliffs, N. J.: Prentice-Hall, 1969.

Raup, H. F. "The Fence in the Cultural Landscape." *Western Folklore* 6 (1947):1–7.

Read, Allen Walker. "The Pronunciation of the Word 'Missouri.'" *American Speech* 8 (December 1933): 22–36.

Richmond, W. Edson, ed. *Studies in Folklore, in Honor of Distinguished Service Professor Stith Thompson*. Bloomington: Indiana University Press, 1957.

Riedl, Norbert F. "Folklore and the Study of Material Aspects of Folk Culture." *Journal of American Folklore* 79:314 (1966): 557–63.

———. "Folklore vs. 'Volkskunde.'" *Tennessee Folklore Society Bulletin* 21:2 (June 1965): 47–53.

Riedl, Norbert F.; Ball, Donald B.; and Cavender, Anthony P. *A Survey of Traditional Architecture and Related Material Folk Culture Patterns in the Normandy Reservoir, Coffee County, Tennessee*. Knoxville: University of Tennessee Department of Anthropology Report on Investigation No. 17, 1976.

Riedl, Norbert F., and Buckles, Carol K. "House Customs and Beliefs in East Tennessee." In Charles H. Faulkner and Carol K. Buckles, eds., *Glimpses of Southern Appalachian Folk Culture: Papers in Memory of Norbert F. Riedl*, pp. 43–55. Knoxville: Tennessee Anthropological Association Miscellaneous Paper No. 3, 1978.

Riviere, G. H. "Folk Architecture—Past, Present and Future." *Landscape* 4:1 (Summer 1954): 5–12.

Roberts, Leonard W. *South from Hell-fer-Sartin*. Berea, Ky.: Council of the Southern Mountains, 1964.

Roberts, Warren E. "Some Comments on Log Construction in Scandinavia and in the United States." In Linda Dégh, Henry Glassie, and Felix J. Oinas, eds., *Folklore Today: A Festschrift for Richard M. Dorson*, pp. 437–50. Bloomington: Indiana University Press, 1976.

Rouse, Irving. "Culture Areas and Co-Tradition." *Southwestern Journal of Anthropology* 13:2 (1957): 122–33.

Sanders, Gordon R. "A Survey of the Vocabulary of Seven North East Missouri Counties." Master's thesis, University of Missouri, 1957.

Sauer, Carl Ortwin. *The Geography of the Ozark Highlands of Missouri*. Chicago: University of Chicago Press, 1920.

Schofield, Edna. "The Evolution and Development of Tennessee Houses." *Journal of the*

Tennessee Academy of Sciences 11:4 (October 1936): 229–40.

Schoolcraft, Henry Rowe. *Journal of a Tour into the Interior of Missouri and Arkansaw, from Potosi, or Mine a Burton, in a Southwest Direction, toward the Rocky Mountains, Performed in the years 1818 and 1819.* London: Sir Richard Phillips and Co., 1821.

———. *Travels in the Central Portions of the Mississippi Valley: Comprising Observations on its Mineral Geography, Internal Resources, and its Aborigine Population.* New York: Collins and Hannay, 1825.

Semple, Ellen Churchill. *American History and Its Geographic Conditions.* Boston: Houghton Mifflin, 1903.

———. "The Anglo-Saxons of the Kentucky Mountains: A Study in Anthropogeography." *The Geographical Journal* 17 (1901): 588–623.

Settle, William Anderson, Jr. *Jesse James Was His Name.* Columbia: University of Missouri Press, 1966.

Shalhope, Robert E. *Sterling Price: Portrait of a Southerner.* Columbia: University of Missouri Press, 1971.

Shaw, Earl B. *Anglo-America: A Regional Geography.* New York: John Wiley, 1957.

Shoemaker. A. L., ed. *The Pennsylvania Barn.* Kutztown, Pa.: Pennsylvania Folklife Society, 1955.

Shoemaker, Floyd C. "Missouri—Heir of Southern Tradition and Individuality." *Missouri Historical Review* 36:4 (July 1942): 435–36.

———. *Missouri and Missourians: Land of Contrasts and People of Achievement.* Chicago: Lewis Publishing Co., 1943.

Shoemaker, Floyd C., ed. *Missouri Day by Day.* 2 vols. Columbia: State Historical Society of Missouri, 1942.

Shoemaker, Floyd C., et al. *The Messages and Proclamations of the Governors of the state of Missouri.* 12 vols. Columbia: State Historical Society of Missouri, 1922–1930.

Shull, Bettie B. "A Survey of the Vocabulary of Eight Western Missouri Counties." Master's thesis, University of Missouri, 1953.

Shurtleff, Harold R. *The Log Cabin Myth: A Study of the Early Dwellings of the English Colonists in North America.* Cambridge, Mass.: Harvard University Press, 1939.

Simpkins, Francis B. *A History of the South.* New York: 1963.

Sloane, Eric. *An Age of Barns.* New York: Ballantine Books, 1974.

Smith, Henry Nash. *Virgin Land.* Cambridge, Mass.: Harvard University Press, 1950.

Smith, J. T. "The Concept of Diffusion in Its Application to Vernacular Building." In J. Geraint Jenkins, ed., *Studies in Folklife: Essays in Honor of Iorwerth C. Peate*, pp. 60–78. New York: Barnes and Noble, 1969.

———. "The Dating of Buildings: Problems and Fallacies." *Vernacular Architecture* 3 (1972): 16–20.

———. "The Evolution of the English Peasant House to the late Seventeenth Century: The Evidence of the Buildings." *Journal of the British Archaeological Association* 33 (1970): 122–47.

Smith, Peter. *Houses of the Welsh Countryside: A Study in Historical Geography.* London: Her Majesty's Stationary Office, 1975.

Smith, Peter C., and Raitz, Karl B. "Negro Hamlets and Agricultural Estates in Kentucky's Inner Bluegrass." *Geographical Review* 64:2 (1974): 217–34.

Spencer, J. E., and Horvath, Ronald J. "How Does an Agricultural Region Originate?" *Annals of the Association of American Geographers* 53 (1963): 74–92.

Stampp, Kenneth M. *The Peculiar Institution.* New York: Random House, 1956.

State Historical Society of Missouri, comp. *Historic Missouri.* Columbia: State Historical Society of Missouri, 1959.

Stell, Christopher. "Pennine Houses: An Introduction." *Folk Life* 3 (1965): 5–24.

Stevens, W. B. *Centennial History of Missouri, 1820–1921.* 4 vols. St. Louis: S. J. Clarke Publishing Co., 1921.

Steward, Julian. *Theory of Culture Change.* Urbana: University of Illinois Press, 1955.

Stewart, George R. *U.S. 40: Cross Section of the United States of America*. Boston: Houghton Mifflin Co., 1953.

Stotz, Charles Morse. *The Early Architecture of Western Pennsylvania*. New York: William Helburn, 1936.

Sturtevant, William C. *Guide to Field Collecting of Ethnographic Specimens*. Washington, D.C.: Smithsonian Institution Museum of Natural History, 1967.

Swaim, Doug, ed. *Carolina Dwelling*. Raleigh: North Carolina State University School of Design Student Publication, vol. 26, 1978.

Swanton, John R. *Indian Tribes of North America*. Washington, D.C.: Bureau of American Ethnology, Bulletin 145, 1952.

Switzler, William F. *History of Boone County, Missouri*. St. Louis: Western Historical Co., 1882.

———. *History of Missouri*. St. Louis, 1897.

Symons, Harry. *Fences*. Toronto: Ryerson Press, 1952.

Syndor, Charles S. *The Development of Southern Sectionalism, 1819–1848*. Baton Rouge: Louisiana State University Press, 1948.

Talpaler, Morris. *The Sociology of Colonial Virginia*. New York: Philosophical Library, 1960.

Taylor, Carl C., et al. *Rural Life in the United States*. New York: Alfred A. Knopf, 1949.

Taylor, William R. *Cavalier and Yankee: The Old South and American National Character*. New York: Braziller, 1961.

Tebbetts, Diane. "Traditional Houses of Independence County, Arkansas." *Pioneer America* 10:1 (June 1978): 37–55.

Thomas, C. "Archaeology and Folk-Life Studies." *Gwerin* 3:1 (June 1950): 7–17.

Thompson, George B. "Folk Culture and the People." *The Advancement of Science* 14:57 (June 1958): 480–86.

Thwaites, Reuben Gold, ed. *Early Western Travels, 1748–1846. . . .* 32 vols. Cleveland: A. H. Clark Co., 1904–1907.

Toelken, Barre. *The Dynamics of Folklore*. Boston: Houghton Mifflin, 1979.

Trewartha, G. T. "Some Regional Characteristics of American Farmsteads." *Annals of the Association of American Geographers* 38:3 (September 1948): 169–225.

Trexlar, Harrison A. "The Value and Sale of the Missouri Slave." *Missouri Historical Review* 8 (1914): 69–85.

Trindell, Roger T. "American Folklore Studies and Geography." *Southern Folklore Quarterly* 34:1 (1970): 1–11.

———. "Building in Brick in Early America." *The Geographical Review* 58:3 (1968): 484–87.

Trombly, Albert E. *Little Dixie*. Columbia: University of Missouri Press, 1955.

Tuan, Yi-Fu. "Geography, Phenomenology, and the Study of Human Nature." *Canadian Journal of Geography* 15:3 (1971): 181–92.

Tupes, Herschel. "The Influence of Slavery upon Missouri Politics (to Include 1860)." Master's thesis, University of Missouri, 1910.

Twain, Mark. *The Adventures of Huckleberry Finn*. Scranton, Pa.: Chandler Facsimile Edition, 1962.

United States Record and Pension Office. *Missouri Troops in Service During the Civil War*. Washington, D.C.: U.S. Government Printing Office, 1902.

Upton, Dell. "Board Roofing in Tidewater Virginia." *APT Bulletin* 8:4 (1976): 22–43.

———. "Toward a Performance Model of Vernacular Architecture: Early Tidewater Virginia as a Case Study." *Folklore Forum* 12:2–3 (1979): 173–98.

Utz, Cornelius. "Life in Missouri, 1800–1840, as Pictured in Travelers' Accounts, Letters and Journals." Master's thesis, University of Missouri, 1933.

Vance, Rupert. *Human Geography of the South: A Study in Regional Resources and Human Adequacy*. Chapel Hill: University of North Carolina Press, 1935.

VanNada, M. L., ed. *The Book of Missourians*. New York: D.C. Heath and Co., 1918.

van Ravenswaay, Charles. *The Arts and Architecture of German Settlements in Missouri: A Survey of a Vanishing Culture*. Columbia: University of Missouri Press, 1977.

van Wagenen, Jared, Jr. *The Golden Age of Homespun*. New York: Hill and Wang, 1953.

Violette, Eugene M. *A History of Missouri*. New York: D.C. Heath and Co., 1918.

Vlach, John Michael. "'The Candada Homestead': A Saddlebag Log House in Monroe County, Indiana." *Pioneer America* 4:2 (July 1972): 8–17.

von Sydow, Carl W. *Selected Papers on Folklore*. Copenhagen: Rosenkilde and Bagger, 1948.

Wacker, Peter O. "Cultural and Commercial Regional Associations of Traditional Smokehouses in New Jersey." *Pioneer America* 3:2 (July 1971): 25–34.

———. "Folk Architecture as an Indicator of Culture Areas and Culture Diffusion: Dutch Barns and Barracks in New Jersey." *Pioneer America* 5:2 (July 1973): 37–47.

———. *The Musconetcong Valley of New Jersey: A Historical Geography*. New Brunswick, N.J.: Rutgers University Press, 1968.

Walker, H. J., and Haag, W. G., eds. *Man and Cultural Heritage: Papers in Honor of Fred B. Kniffen*. Baton Rouge: Louisiana State University School of Geoscience, 1974.

Wallace, A. F. C. *Religion: An Anthropological View*. New York: Harcourt, Brace, 1966.

———. "Revitalization Movements." *American Anthropologist* 58 (1956): 264–81.

Waller, Alexander H. *History of Randolph County, Missouri*. Cleveland and Topeka: Historical Publishing Co., 1920.

Ware, C. F., ed. *The Cultural Approach to History*. New York: Columbia University Press, 1940.

Waterhouse, Sylvester. *The Resources of Missouri*. St. Louis: Aug. Wiebusch and Son, 1867.

Waterman, Thomas Tileston. *The Dwellings of Colonial America*. Chapel Hill: University of North Carolina Press, 1950.

Watkins, Floyd C., and Watkins, Charles Hubert. *Yesterday in the Hills*. Athens: University of Georgia Press, 1973.

Watson, J. Wreford. "Image Geography: The Myth of America in the American Scene." *The Advancement of Science* 27 (1970–1971): 1–9.

Weaver, John C. "The Changing Patterns of Cropland Use in the Middle West." *Economic Geography* 30 (1954): 1–47.

Weller, Jack. *Yesterday's People: Life in Contemporary Appalachia*. Lexington: University Press of Kentucky, 1965.

Wellman, Paul I. "Missouri's Little Dixie is Real Enough Although It Appears on No Maps." *Kansas City Times*, 5 December 1941.

Weslager, Charles A. *The Log Cabin in America*. New Brunswick, N. J.: Rutgers University Press, 1969.

Wetmore, Alphonso. *A Gazateer of the State of Missouri, with a Map of the State . . . to Which is Added an Appendix, Containing Frontier Sketches, Etc*. St. Louis: C. Keemle, 1837.

Whitaker, James W., ed. *Farming in the Midwest, 1840–1900*. Washington, D.C.: The Agricultural History Society, 1974.

Whitaker, Russell. "Regional Interdependence." *Journal of Geography* 31 (1932): 154ff.

Wight, Jane. *Brick Building in England, from the Middle Ages to 1550*. London: John Baker, 1972.

Wildhaber, Richard. "A Bibliographical Introduction to American Folklife." *New York Folklore Quarterly* 21:4 (1965): 259–302.

Wiley, Bell Irvin. *The Life of Johnny Reb: The Common Soldier of the Confederacy*. Indianapolis: Bobbs-Merrill, 1943.

Wilhelm, Eugene J., Jr. "Folk Settlement Types in the Blue Ridge Mountains." *Keystone Folklore Quarterly* 12:3 (1971): 154–74.

Wilhelm, Hubert G. H. "Southern Ohio as a Settlement Region: An Historical-Geographical Interpretation." *Proceedings of the Pioneer America Society* 1 (1972): 96–123.

Wilhelm, Hubert G. H., and Miller, Michael. "Half-Timbering Construction: A Relic Building Method in Ohio." *Pioneer America* 6:2 (July 1974): 43–51.

Wiliam, Eurwyn. "Farm Buildings in the Vale of Clwyd, 1550–1800." *Folk Life* 11 (1973): 34–60.

Williams, Roger M. "The Return of the Log House." *Americana* (January–February 1979): 46–53.

Williams, Walter, ed. *A History of Northeast Missouri*. vol. 1. Chicago and New York: Lewis Publishing Co., 1913.

Wilson, Eugene M. *Alabama Folk Houses*. Montgomery: Alabama Historical Commission, 1975.

———. "The Single-Pen Log House in the South." *Pioneer America* 2:1 (1970): 21–28.

———. "Some Similarities between American and European Folk Houses." *Pioneer America* 3:2 (1971): 8–14.

Wilstach, Paul. *Tidewater Virginia*. Indianapolis: Bobbs-Merrill, 1929.

Withers, Robert S. "The Pioneers' First Corn Crop." *Missouri Historical Review* 46 (1951): 39–45.

———. "The Stake and Rider Fence." *Missouri Historical Review* 44:3 (1950): 225–31.

Wittke, Carl. *We Who Built America: The Saga of the Immigrant*. Cleveland: Case Western Reserve University Press, 1939, 1964.

Wolf, Eric R. *Peasants*. Englewood Cliffs, N. J.: Prentice-Hall, 1966.

Wood, Gordon R. *Vocabulary Change: A Study of Variation in Regional Words in Eight of the Southern States*. Carbondale: Southern Illinois University Press, 1971.

Wood-Jones, Raymond B. *Traditional Domestic Architecture in the Banbury Region*. Manchester, Eng.: Manchester University Press, 1963.

Wright, John K. *Human Nature in Geography: Fourteen Papers, 1925–1965*. Cambridge, Mass.: Harvard University Press, 1966.

Wright, Lawrence. *Home Fires Burning: The History of Domestic Heating and Cooking*. London: Routledge and Kegan Paul, 1964.

Wright, M. "The Antecedents of the Double-Pen House Type." *Annals of the Association of American Geographers* 48:2 (1958): 109–17.

Yoder, Don. "The First International Symposium on Ethnological Food Research." *Keystone Folklore Quarterly* 16:4 (1971): 155–63.

———. "Folklife." In Tristram P. Coffin, ed., *American Folklore*, pp. 53–63. Washington, D.C.: U.S. Information Service, 1968.

———. "The Folklife Studies Movement." *Pennsylvania Folklife* 13:3 (1963): 43–56.

———. "Historical Sources for American Foodways Research and Plans for an American Foodways Archive." *Ethnologica Scandinavica* 2 (1971): 41–55.

———. "Historical Sources for American Traditional Cookery." *Pennsylvania Folklife* 22:3 (1971): 16–29.

Zelinsky, Wilbur. *The Cultural Geography of the United States*. Englewood Cliffs, N.J.: Prentice-Hall, 1973.

———. "The Log House in Georgia." *Geographical Review* 43:2 (1953): 173–93.

———. "The New England Connecting Barn." *Geographical Review* 48:4 (1962): 540–53.

———. "Walls and Fences." *Landscape* 8:3 (1959): 14–20.

———. "Where the South Begins: The Northern Limits of the Cis-Appalachian South in Terms of Settlement Landscape." *Social Forces* 30:2 (1951): 172–78.

Index